Introduction

Welcome to the world of MS-DOS 6.22! This book is your modern comprehensive guide, to revisit the golden age of personal computers. Released in June of 1994 , MS-DOS 6.22 marked a significant chapter in the evolution of personal computers. While its command-line interface may seem like a stark contrast to the user-friendly graphical interfaces of today, understanding MS-DOS offers a unique window into the past and a deeper appreciation for the technological advancements we enjoy today.

This book isn't just about installing MS-DOS; it's about reliving the excitement and wonder of early personal computers. Imagine the thrill of powering on your first machine, the whirring of the fan, and the anticipation as the familiar green text filled the screen. Remember the boundless exploration, discovering the capabilities hidden within your machine, venturing forth to conquer new programs and games. Each successful hurdle, each mastered software, and every customized setting brought a surge of accomplishment, a testament to your growing knowledge and control.

Through this journey back in time, you'll rediscover the awe-inspiring moment you first powered on your machine, recalling the unfamiliar sights and sounds, the excitement of navigating a new digital world, and the potential it held. Rediscover the joy of tinkering, the thrill of troubleshooting hardware issues, configuring software settings, and customizing your system into a unique reflection of your preferences. Embrace the hands-on learning, the satisfaction of trial and error, and the sense of accomplishment that comes with mastering new skills.

This journey back isn't just about nostalgia, it's about appreciating the ingenuity and resourcefulness of the era. Witness how developers and users pushed the boundaries of technology with creative solutions and workarounds, demonstrating how limitations often sparked innovation and forced users to think outside the box to achieve their goals. By understanding the foundation that paved the way for today's technology, you'll gain not only a sense of wonder but also a deeper appreciation of computing history .

Experience the thrill of hands-on computing:

Modern computing often feels like a point-and-click journey, with limited opportunities for direct interaction. MS-DOS, however, offers a refreshing and empowering alternative. It's an invitation to step away from the pre-defined menus and icons and embrace the world of the command line. Here, you'll communicate directly with your computer using concise and powerful commands, fostering a deeper understanding and unmediated control over your system.

Immerse yourself in the directness and efficiency of the command line. Learn to navigate folders with ease, launch programs with a single line of text, and configure your system precisely according to your needs. Unlike the often-opaque behavior of modern interfaces, MS-DOS provides instant feedback. Every command you enter unfolds its impact on the screen, allowing you to witness the inner workings of your computer in real-time. This immediate feedback loop becomes a valuable learning tool, enabling you to quickly grasp cause and effect and learn from your mistakes in a safe environment.

Beyond the practical benefits, MS-DOS empowers you with a unique skillset. Mastering the command line equips you with the ability to navigate and manipulate files and directories using text-based commands. This skillset forms the foundation for understanding how operating systems organize and manage data, providing valuable insights that transcend the limitations of MS-DOS. It offers a deeper appreciation for the workings of modern graphical interfaces and equips you with knowledge that can be applied across various computing systems.

By embracing the hands-on experience of MS-DOS, you'll gain more than just the ability to install and configure an old operating system. You'll develop valuable problem-solving skills, cultivate a deeper understanding of computer architecture, and unlock a powerful tool for interacting with technology in a more direct and meaningful way.

Successfully installing, configuring, and using MS-DOS 6.22 provides a tangible sense of achievement and a deeper understanding of how computers truly work. Regardless of your motivation, this book equips you with the knowledge and skills necessary to embark on a rewarding journey. Through clear step-by-step instructions and practical advice. you'll gain the ability to:

- Install and configure MS-DOS 6.22 on physical or virtual environments.

- Navigate the command line interface with confidence.
- Optimize your system for performance and stability.

- Install and run classic MS-DOS applications and explore the vast world of retrocomputing.

So, grab your keyboard, prepare for a unique learning experience, and get ready to unlock the secrets of MS-DOS 6.22!

Prerequisites

Old hardware - While there is no single "ideal" hardware configuration for a dedicated MS-DOS PC, the recommended approach is to begin with the software you intend to run and then select hardware accordingly. Many enthusiasts consider a 486 DX2/66 MHz processor to be an excellent choice, while others advocate for early Pentium processors with clock speeds ranging from 133 to 200 MHz. The below table provides a general guideline for compatibility. Specific game requirements may vary.

Game Type	Minimum CPU	Notes
Classic Text-	Any 8086 or higher	These games rely primarily on text

Based Adventures		processing and require minimal processing power.
Early DOS Games (1980s)	8086 (286 preferred)	Games from this era were designed for lower clock speeds. A 286 CPU offers a smoother experience.
DOS Games (Early 1990s)	386 (486 preferred)	As graphics and sound capabilities increased, a 386 became the baseline. A 486 provides better performance.
DOS Games (Mid-1990s)	486 DX2/66 MHz (Pentium 133 MHz preferred)	Games became more demanding during this period. A 486 DX2/66 is a good starting point, with Pentium CPUs offering a significant performance boost.

However, if your primary concern is simply running MS-DOS 6.22 and you're not particularly invested in specific software compatibility beyond that, the presence of ISA slots on the motherboard offers a general indicator of compatibility. These slots were commonly found in computers manufactured between the late 1980s and early 2000s, and their presence usually suggests the system can handle MS-DOS 6.22.

It is important to note, however, that ISA slots are not a guaranteed indicator of compatibility. Other factors, such as the specific processor, memory capacity, and other hardware components, can still play a role. For the most accurate assessment of compatibility, it is always advisable to consult the system's documented specifications or conduct further research specific to the hardware in question.

One 8-bit and five 16-bit ISA slots on a motherboard

A 3.5-inch floppy disk drive: This drive serves as the primary medium for transferring the operating system files from the installation diskettes to your computer's hard disk. While some alternative installation methods might exist for certain configurations, the floppy disk drive remains the most reliable and widely supported approach for MS-DOS 6.22.

O ne floppy diskette (two or more recommended) : While technically only one diskette is strictly necessary for installation, it is strongly recommended to have at least two. This redundancy provides a valuable safeguard in case of unforeseen issues during the installation process, such as a corrupted diskette or an unexpected error.

MS-DOS 6.22 installation diskettes: These diskettes, typically sold as a set, contain the necessary files and instructions for installing the operating system on your machine. If possible, I suggest using or tracking down any original installation media you may have had or picking up a set on eBay - While original installation media, particularly boxed sets, hold a certain nostalgic charm, acquiring them can be challenging. Fortunately, the diskettes themselves are often readily available and at an affordable price

Patience: This journey into the world of MS-DOS is one that requires patience, a spirit of exploration, and a willingness to confront challenges head-on. Be prepared to dedicate time and effort, as unforeseen obstacles are likely to arise along the way. Remember, the process itself is an enlightening experience, and approaching it with discontentment at every hurdle will diminish the enjoyment significantly.

While I aim to provide comprehensive guidance throughout this project, familiarity with the command line interface (CLI) is recommended. Though I believe most of the journey can be navigated without extensive prior experience, a basic understanding of CLI commands will be an invaluable asset. Remember, frustration is a natural companion on the path of learning. Should you encounter setbacks, approach them with a calm mind and a willingness to troubleshoot. This is an opportunity to hone your problem-solving skills and deepen your understanding of the intricate workings of MS-DOS. Embrace the challenges and view them as opportunities to learn and troubleshoot, ultimately fostering a deeper understanding of this historic operating system.

Hard Disk Preparation

Before installing MS-DOS 6.22, it may be necessary to partition and format your hard disk. This process prepares the storage space for the operating system by dividing it into logical sections and establishing a file system. Should you need to partition and format your hard disk, follow these steps:

1. Boot your computer using the first installation disk (Disk 1).

2. Upon reaching the MS-DOS Setup welcome screen, press the F3 key. This action will bypass the installer and navigate you directly to the MS-DOS command prompt.

3. To repartition your hard disk, execute the FDISK command. This powerful utility allows you to manage disk partitions, including creating, deleting, and modifying them.

```
                        MS-DOS Version 6
                     Fixed Disk Setup Program
                (C)Copyright Microsoft Corp. 1983 - 1993

                          FDISK Options

   Current fixed disk drive: 1

   Choose one of the following:

   1. Create DOS partition or Logical DOS Drive
   2. Set active partition
   3. Delete partition or Logical DOS Drive
   4. Display partition information


   Enter choice: [1]




   Press Esc to exit FDISK
```

4. Within the FDISK program, utilize option 3 to eliminate any existing partitions that are no longer needed. Subsequently, employ option 1 to establish new partitions on your hard disk.

5. It is crucial to note that MS-DOS 6.x is only capable of recognizing FAT16 partitions, which possess a maximum size limitation of 2 gigabytes (GB).

6. If necessary, utilize option 2 on your C: drive to specifically mark it as the "boot" partition. This designates the drive from which MS-DOS will load upon system startup.

7. Be advised that once you finalize any alterations within FDISK, you will be prompted to reboot your computer for the changes to take effect.

To prepare your hard disk drive for MS-DOS 6.22, you will need to format it. This process erases all existing data and prepares the drive for use with the operating system. At the command prompt enter the following command, replacing labelname with your desired volume label (optional):

```
FORMAT /V:labelname /U /S C:
```

Explanation of flags:

/V : Sets t he volume label for the drive, which appears when browsing directories. This step is optional.

/U : Performs an unconditional format, erasing all data and bypassing any confirmation prompts. This is recommended to ensure a clean installation.

/S : Copies the necessary DOS system files to the partition, allowi ng it to boot independently.

Formatting Additional Partitions:

If your ha rd drive contains multiple partitions, you need to format them individually using the same command. However, omit the /s flag for subsequent partitions as they won't re quire bootable system files.

Once all partitions are formatted, run `setup.exe` from the installation media to continue the installation process. This step guides you through installing the remaining MS-DOS components and configuration options.

Note: Formatting permanently erases all data on the chosen drive. Ensure you have backed up any important information before proceeding.

Installing MS-DOS 6.22: Step-by-Step

Before embarking on this installation journey, ensure you have the necessary software:

- **MS-DOS 6.22 Setup:** This free upgrade transforms existing MS-DOS 6.x installations (including version 6.2 on your system) to the latest 6.22 iteration.

- **MS-DOS 6.22 Supplemental Utilities (Optional):** This package contains additional utilities, drivers, and programs not included in the base installation, potentially enticing the curious. However, it's not essential for core functionality.

- It's worth noting that formatting your hard drive with `FDISK` and `FORMAT` might be necessary, but the core installation process is remarkably straightforward.

1. If you haven't initiated the process yet, begin by booting your computer using the first

MS-DOS 6.22 installation disk.

2. Upon successful boot, press the Enter key to commence the setup process.

```
Microsoft MS-DOS 6.22 Setup
═══════════════════════════════

        Welcome to Setup.

        The Setup program prepares MS-DOS 6.22 to run on your
        computer.

           • To set up MS-DOS now, press ENTER.

           • To learn more about Setup before continuing, press F1.

           • To exit Setup without installing MS-DOS, press F3.

        Note: If you have not backed up your files recently, you
              might want to do so before installing MS-DOS. To back
              up your files, press F3 to quit Setup now. Then, back
              up your files by using a backup program.

        To continue Setup, press ENTER.


ENTER=Continue  F1=Help  F3=Exit  F5=Remove Color  F7=Install to a Floppy Disk
```

3. If you pre-formatted the installation disks as instructed, the installer might identify an existing DOS version. In this scenario, select "Continue Setup and replace your current version of DOS" to proceed with the replacement.

4. S et the date, time, country, and keyboard layout options to align with your preferences. Once satisfied, choose "The settings are correct" to move forward.

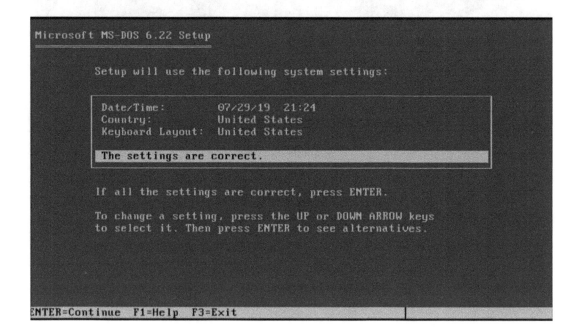

5. It's recommended to choose the default installation directory of C:\DOS. Simply press

Enter to continue.

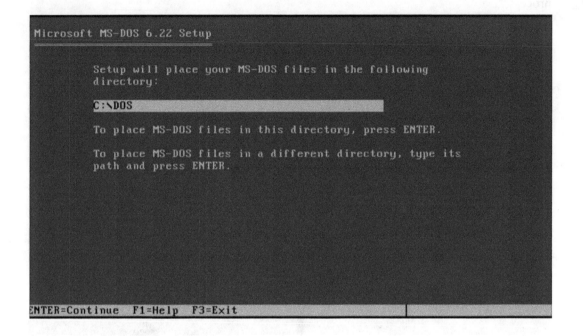

```
Microsoft MS-DOS 6.22 Setup

        Setup will place your MS-DOS files in the following
        directory:

        C:\DOS

        To place MS-DOS files in this directory, press ENTER.

        To place MS-DOS files in a different directory, type its
        path and press ENTER.




ENTER=Continue   F1=Help   F3=Exit
```

6. Follow the on-screen prompts to switch disks twice as instructed by the installer. After the final disk switch, the system will automatically reboot to finalize the installation process.

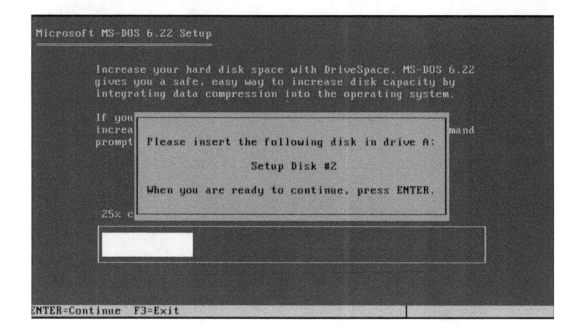

7. Upon rebooting, you'll be greeted by a clean and basic DOS environment, ready for your exploration.

Congratulations! You've successfully installed MS-DOS 6.22 and can now navigate the world of this classic operating system.

Upgrading from Prior MS-DOS Versions (Optional)

This sect ion details the optional upgrade process for users who have previously installed versions of MS-DOS 6.0, 6.2, or 6.21. While upgrading to MS-DOS 6.22 Set-Up is not strictly mandatory, it's highly recommended due to the numerous benefits and improvements it offers.

One hurdle you might encounter during the upgrade process is transferring the STEPUP files to your DOS system. These files exceed the capacity of a single floppy disk and are typically designed for direct download and execution on the target computer – a challenge for a freshly installed MS-DOS lacking internet access.

To overcome this obstacle, I suggest the following steps:

1. Downloa d and unpack the STEPUP.EXE file o n your primary computer with internet access.
2. Manually create a set of three floppy disks w ith the following distribution:

Disk 1:

```
SETUP.BAT
README.NOW
```

```
1MSDOS62.EXE
```

Disk 2:

```
2MSDOS62.EXE
```

Disk 3:

```
3MSDOS62.EXE
```

3. On your DOS System, create a dedicated directory to store the Set-Up files. This directory will serve as a repository for these files, allowing you to easily reinstall the upgrade without requiring repeated diskette copying in future installations. Here's how to create the directory:

```
MKDIR C:\BACKUP

MKDIR C:\BACKUP\STEPUP
```

4. Alternatively, i f you have sufficient hard drive space, consider creatin g a separate D: drive specifically for backups and data storage. This allows you to reinstall MS-DOS by formatting only the C: drive while preserving your essential files, drivers, and configurations on the D: drive. Here's how to create the D: drive (consult your system's documentation for detailed instructions):

5. Use the COPY command to transfer the upgrade files from each floppy disk to your dedicated backup directory:

```
COPY A:\*.* C:\BACKUP\STEPUP
```

6. Create a temporary directory on your C: drive to house the Set-Up files during the upgrade process. This directory can be deleted once the upgrade is complete:

```
MKDIR C:\STEPUP
```

7. Copy the entir e C:\BACKUP\STEPUP direc tory to the newly created
temporary directory:

```
COPY C:\BACKUP\SETUP C:\STEPUP
```

By following these steps, you'll successfully transfer the MS-DOS 6.22 Set-Up files to your

system, preparing you for the actual upgrade process. Remember, the provided instructions

aim to be clear and concise, but always refer to the official documentation for specific

details and potential variations depending on your system configuration.

To upgrade your existing installation of MS-DOS to version 6.22, follow these steps:

1. At the command prompt type `CD C:\STEPUP`

2. Execute the `STEPUP.BAT` script by typing its name and pressing Enter.
3. Press Y to signify your acceptance of the End User License Agreement (EULA).
4. Press Y again to confirm that C: is the drive where your existing MS-DOS
   installation resides.
5. At the Welcome screen, press F3 to exit the initial setup process.
6. Execute the `STEPUP.EXE /G` com mand to initiate the unattended upgrade
   process, bypassing the creation of uninstall floppy disks.
7. Press Enter at the Welcome screen to continue. Then, press Enter again to confirm
   your existing system settings.
8. Press Y to commence the upgrade process.
9. Once the upgrade completes, the system will prompt you to reboot. Do so and
   verify the successful installation by running the ver command at the command
   prompt. This command should display the version information, confirming that you
   are now running MS-DOS 6.22.

10. Finally, you can safely remove the SETUP directory and any remaining files from
    your previous MS-DOS installation using the following commands:

```
DELTREE /Y C:\STEP UP


DEL OLDDOS
```

Note: Th e DELTREE /Y command permanently deletes the specified directory and all its contents, so use it with caution. The DEL OLDDOS command might need to be replaced with the specific name of the directory containing your old MS-DOS files if it differs from "OLDDOS".

MS-DOS 6.22 Supplemental Utilities

While the core functionalities of MS-DOS 6.22 provide a robust foundation, the "MS-DOS 6.2 Supplemental Utilities" disk offers an optional treasure trove of additional features. Though not necessary, these utilities can enhance your experience by reintroducing functionalities present in earlier DOS versions and offering a glimpse into the evolution of user interfaces.

Installation:

1. Insert the diskette and execute   A :\STEPUP.BAT C:\DOS to in itiate the installation process.

2. Select "S" to choose specific components.

3. Respond with "Y" or "N" for each listed component   based on your preferences. This guide highlights two noteworthy options:

Additional MS-DOS Utilities:

This selection unlocks various tools, potentially including utilities for disk management, file compression, and text manipulation.

A Nostalgic Gem: QBasic Nibbles

One particularly captivating addition within the "Additional MS-DOS Utilities" is QBasic

Nibbles. This seemingly simple game, reminiscent of the classic "Snake," offers hours of

addictive entertainment and evokes a sense of nostalgia for those familiar with its charm

from earlier DOS experiences. To embark on this nostalgic journey, simply execute

```
QBASIC.EXE /RUN C:\DOS\NIBBLES.BAS
```

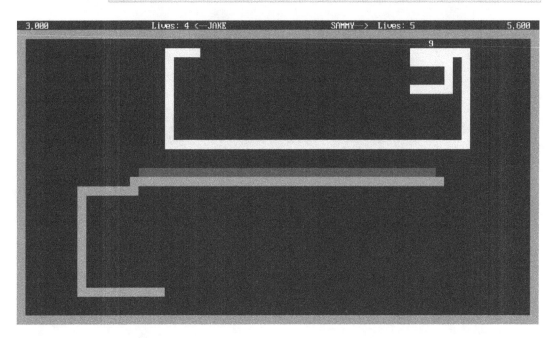

Exploring the MS-DOS Shell (DOSSHELL):

While not the primary focus of this exploration into MS-DOS, DOSSHELL merits attention for its historical significance and innovative appro ach. This primitive GUI, often dubbed "Windows Light," operates atop DOS, offering functionalities like:

- **File management:** Navigate folders and files visually.

- **File associations:** Link specific file types to corresponding applications for automatic execution.
- **Menu-driven task list:** Launch applications and switch between them conveniently.

- **Pseudo-multitasking:** Manage multiple programs seemingly running concurrently (limitations apply).

It's important to acknowledge that running a full-fledged Windows environment like Windows 3.x would provide a considerably more powerful and versatile user experience. However, DOSSHELL represents a fascinating historical stepping stone and a testament to the ingenuity of early interface designers.

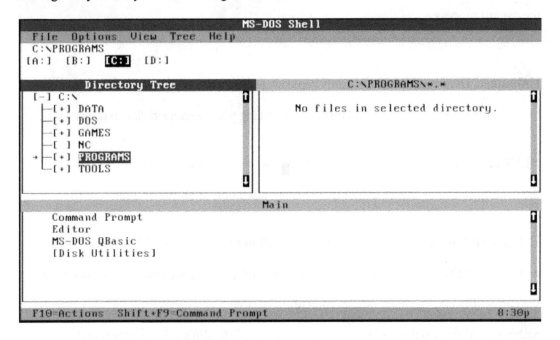

DOSSHELL Tips (Optional):

Execution Modes: Choose between text mode (`DOSSHELL.EXE /T`) and GUI mode (`DOSSHLL.EXE /G`).

Enhanced Resolution: Utilize GUI mode with the `/G:H2` parameter to experience a higher resolution display.

Customizing the Program List: Modify the program list displayed at the bottom of the interface through the GUI or by editing the dosshell.ini file, drawing inspiration from the existing menu items.

Configuring Your DOS Environment

Here's how to establish a functional workspace for your DOS experience. This stage involves setting up essential directories and installing helpful utilities that will streamline the overall process.

Enhanced DOSKEY: This utility replaces the standard DOSKEY, offering features like tab completion and command history, enhancing your command-line experience.

PEDIT: This enhanced text editor offers a more user-friendly experience compared to the default EDIT command, enabling easier manipulation of DOS configuration files.

INFO-ZIP UnZip: This open-source tool allows you to extract ZIP archives directly within your DOS environment, aiding in the installation of various programs. Downloading the correct file can be cumbersome, so here's a reliable link: [insert link]. While other archiving utilities exist with broader format support, Info-Zip's ease of access and proficiency in handling the most common DOS program formats makes it a suitable choice for this setup.

Creating a Functional Workspace:

Before moving on, let's establish a well-organized environment:

1. Use the `CD C:\` com mand to navigate to the C drive's root directory.
2. Use the following commands to establish directories for specific purposes:

   `MKDIR APPS` : This directory will house your personally installed applications.

> `MKDIR TEMP` : This directory serves as a temporary workspace for some applications.
> `MKDIR BACKUP` : (if necessary): This directory, if needed, will store backups of your original setup files or drivers.

3. Utilize the `PATH C:\APPS;C:\DOS` command to modify the search path. This prioritizes applications residing within your apps directory over the built-in ones residing in the dos directory.

To streamline the installation process for subsequent applications, I highly recommend installing the aforementioned utilities: Enhanced DOSKEY and Pedit. While obtaining and transferring these files to your DOS system can be a temporary inconvenience, the easiest method at this stage is to extract them on your main computer and transfer them via floppy disks. Additionally, it's advisable to create a backup copy of your installation media, files, and drivers under the `C:\BACKUP` directory (ideally in `D:\BACKUP` for easy future access).

Following these steps will establish a well-organized work environment and provide you with essential utilities for a smoother DOS experience. Remember, this document serves as a general guide, and specific steps might require adjustments based on your individual setup and preferences.

Enhancing Your MS-DOS Experience:

This section delves into the installation and configuration of two valuable software utilities designed to elevate your MS-DOS experience: Enhanced DOSKEY and Pedit.

Enhanced DOSKEY:

1. Locate a copy of the `DOSKEY.COM` file. Reliable sources for acquiring such software include reputable online repositories or potentially software compilation discs distributed by user groups or computer magazines.

2. Navigate to the directory containing the `DOSKEY.COM` file using the cd command.

3. Execute the following command to copy the file to the `C:\APPS` dire ctory:

```
COPY DOSKEY.COM C:\APPS
```

4. Once copied, run the following command to activate Enhanced DOSKEY: `C:\APPS\DOSKEY.COM -I`
5. To unlock additional functionalities and usage details, execute the command `DOSKEY -?` at the command prompt. This will display a comprehensive help guide outlining the available options and syntax for utilizing Enhanced DOSKEY effectively.

Pedit text editor:

Acquiring Pedit: You have the option to choose between two versions of Pedit:

`PEDITLGT.EXE` : This version offers a lighter footprint and is recommended for basic editing tasks.
`PEDIT.EXE` : This version provides additional features such as a spell checker and thesaurus, catering to a broader range of editing needs.

Installation:

1. Locate the desired version of Pedit (either `PEDITLGT.EXE` or `PEDIT.EXE`).
2. Navigate to the directory containing the chosen Pedit file using the cd command.
3. Execute the following command to copy the file to the `C:\APPS` dir ectory:

```
For PEDITLGT : COPY PEDITLGT.EXE C:\APPS
For PEDIT: COPY PEDIT.EXE C:\APPS
```

To streamline your experience, consider the following command: `MOVE C:\APPS\PEDITLGT.EXE C:\APPS\EDIT.EXE` This command renames `PEDITLGT.EXE` to `EDIT.EXE` within the `C:\APPS` directory. As a result, you can now launch Pedit simply by typing edit at the command prompt, effectively replacing the built-in DOS editor with Pedit for a more enhanced editing experience.

Customizing Pedit:

1. Launch Pedit by typing edit at the command prompt.

2. If prompted to open a file upon launch, press the Esc key to bypass this prompt and access the configuration menu.
3. Press the Alt key followed by F1 to open the Pedit configuration menu.

4. While personal preferences may vary, here are some recommended non-default settings for an optimal Pedit experience:

Editor Style: Select "2.0" for a user-friendly editing mode.

Scroll Bar: Choose the "dark on light" option (the first pattern after "none") for enhanced visibility during scrolling.

Text Color: Set the text color to "07" (light gray) for improved readability.

Background Color: Choose "01" (black) for a clear background contrast.

Display Options: Enable "Show Char Under Cursor" and "Show Insert Mode" for additional editing cues.

Tab Settings: Set both "Tab Size" and "Tab Expand Size" to "4" for consistent tab behavior.

Function Key Customization: Disable "F2 is File-Save" to prevent accidental overwrites and utilize the dedicated menu options for saving.

Menu Navigation: Enable "Alt Highlights Menu Choices" for easier menu navigation using the Alt key.

Saving Preferences: Enable both "Save Changed Settings" and "Also Save Changed Margins" to preserve your preferred configuration for future use.

5. Once you have adjusted the settings to your liking, press the Esc key followed by Alt and X to exit the configuration menu and save the changes.

By following these steps, you will have successfully installed and configured both Enhanced DOSKEY and Pedit, empowering you to navigate the command line with greater efficiency and enhance your text editing experience within the MS-DOS environment.

Installing and Configuring Tools for a Smoother DOS Experience

This section outlines the installation and configuration of essential utilities for enhancing your DOS environment.

Extracting Compressed Files : Download the `UNZIP.EXE` file and copy it to the `C:\APPS` directory. This basic version provides sufficient functionality for extracting ZIP archives within DOS. Note that `UNZIP32.EXE` offers more features but requires a separate DPMI memory manager, which falls outside the scope of this guide. Other included utilities offer additional functionalities not necessary for basic ZIP extraction.

Important Tip : Frequently editing system configuration files is essential throughout this guide. However, accidental modifications might occasionally lead to boot issues. To recover, as DOS starts booting (when the message "Starting MS-DOS..." appears, usually after the POST beep), press F5 . This initiates a clean boot, bypassing your `AUTOEXEC.BAT` and `CONFIG.SYS` files. Access these files and make necessary corrections to resolve the issue. Reboot your system to load the corrected configuration.

Optimizing Your Autoexec.bat:

1. Navigate to `C:\AUTOEXEC.BAT` a nd modify or add the following lines (leave other settings unchanged for now):

```
LOADHIGH C:\DOS\SMARTDRV.EXE
LOADHIGH C:\APPS\DOSKEY.COM -I
PATH C:\APPS;C:\DOS;C:\DOS\NET
SET DIRCMD=/O:GNE
SET TEMP=C:\TEMP
```

Explanation of Settings:
`LOADHIGH` **:** This command loads device drivers in high memory, increasing available conventional memory for applications.
`C:\DOS\SMARTDRV.EXE` : This is the path to the disk caching utility, improving system performance.
`C:\APPS\DOSKEY.COM -I` : This line loads the DOSKEY command line history and editing tool. The -i option enables case-insensitive history searching.

PATH : This entry defines the directories DOS will search for executable files when you type a command.
SET DIRCMD=/O:GNE : This line sets the default display format for the dir command, providing a cleaner and more informative output.
SET TEMP : This defines the temporary directory used by various applications.

Optimizing the Config File:

The subsequent step involves editing the config.sys file, which houses system configuration settings. Here's a breakdown of the recommended changes:

SWITCHES=/F: This instructs DOS to skip a two-second pause during boot up, reducing the overall boot time. While this slight reduction shortens the window for pressing F5 to initiate a clean boot, it can still be achieved with quick reflexes or by holding down the key before DOS starts loading.

DEVICE=C:\DOS\HIMEM.SYS /TESTMEM:OFF : Thi s line loads the HIMEM.SYS driver, which manages extended memory (upper memory). The /testmem: off parameter skips memory testing during boot, saving time.

DEVICEHIGH=C:\DOS\EMM386.EXE RAM I=B000-B7FF: This activates the EMM386 memory manager, crucial for utilizing the LOADHIGH command and optimizing memo ry usage. The specified parameters configure the memory range for EMM386 operations.

DOS=HIGH,UMB: This line instructs DOS to utilize both upper memory and conventional memory, maximizing available space for applications.

Implementing these adjustments will enhance your MS-DOS experience by optimizing performance, streamlining access to applications, and providing a more convenient user interface. Remember, this is just the initial configuration; further customization options exist to personalize your MS-DOS environment as needed.

Demystifying Memory Management in MS-DOS:

In the realm of MS-DOS, efficient memory management is crucial for unleashing the full potential of your system, especially when running games and applications. This section delves into the key components that govern memory allocation and utilization:

HIMEM.SYS and Extended Memory:

Imagine your computer's memory (RAM) as a vast library. However, by default, MS-DOS can only access the first "shelf" – a limited 640 kilobytes (KB). HIMEM.SYS acts as a skilled librarian, extending your reach beyond this initial shelf and unlocking access to additional memory space – a boon for demanding applications and games. By including the /TESTMEM:OFF option, you avoid unnecessary time spent checking the integrity of your library (RAM) on every boot, streamlining the process.

EMM386.EXE and Expanded Memory:

While HIMEM.SYS provides access to extended memory, EMM386.EXE introduces a further level of organization within this vast space. Think of it as creating designated sections within the library to store specific items (programs and drivers) efficiently. EMM386 enables the use of upper memory (the area between 640 KB and 1 MB) for loading programs and drivers, significantly improving performance and stability.
The RAM option instructs EMM386.EXE to allocate RAM for EMS (Expanded Memory System), an earlier approach to memory management. While superseded by XMS (Extended Memory Specification), EMS remains crucial for many older applications and games discussed in this guide. Unless you have a specific reason, it's recommended to use ram to ensure compatibility with these programs. Further details on EMS can be found in the Addendum.
The I=B000-B7FF option provides an additional space-saving measure by freeing up a small section of memory typically reserved for monochrome monitors, similar to reclaiming seldom-used corners of your library for other purposes.

Upper Memory Blocks and Managing High Memory:

The UMB portion of the DOS option empowers MS-DOS to manage upper memory blocks created by EMM386. This allows commands like LOADHIGH and DEVICEHIGH to function effectively, enabling the loading of programs and drivers into these designated sections for optimal performance. The HIGH option instructs MS-DOS to attempt to store part of itself in high memory when possible, further maximizing available space for your applications and games.

LOADHIGH and DEVICEHIGH:

Imagine having specific tools (programs and drivers) readily available on a workbench (high memory) for immediate use. These commands allow you to strategically store these tools in high memory, ensuring they are easily accessible and don't clutter the main work area (conventional memory).

BREAK and Enabling Program Control:

The `BREAK` c ommand equips you with the essential `CTRL-C` key combination, akin to a safety switch, allowing you to interrupt misbehaving programs and regain control.

`SETVER` and Compatibility: While commented out, the `SETVER` command addresses compatibility with exceptionally old software or drivers not designed specifically for MS-DOS 6.x. If you encounter any compatibility issues, uncommenting this line and consulting Microsoft's resources might be necessary.

Verifying Memory Allocation:

To confirm the effectiveness of your configuration, reboot your system and run the `MEM /C /P` command.   This acts like a library inventory, displaying the utilization of high memory. Ideally, you should see at least some programs listed in the "Upper Memory" column, indicating successful allocation.
By understanding these memory management tools, you empower your MS-DOS system to operate at its full potential, ensuring a smoother and more enjoyable gaming experience.

Network Configuration Options for Your Retro Machine

This section outlines various software options available for establishing network connectivity on your MS-DOS system. Choosing the appropriate software depends on your specific networking needs and desired functionality.

- **Microsoft Network Client 3.0 for MS-DOS:** This software facilitates the mapping of shared drives on Samba or Windows servers, allowing you to access remote files and folders seamlessly. Disks 1 and 2 of your installation media contain the necessary files for this client.

- **NDIS Packet Driver Shim 1.11 :** This software acts as a compatibility layer, enabling the simultaneous use of both Microsoft and non-Microsoft networking utilities on your system. This can be particularly beneficial if you require diverse networking tools. **Note:** To utilize this shim, you will need the `DIS_PKT.ZIP` file.

- **WATTCP (`WAT2002B.ZIP`):** WATTCP is a classic TCP/IP stack for MS-DOS environments. Unlike the other options, WATTCP is typically embedded within the applications that utilize it. This package primarily offers diagnostic applications and comprehensive documentation related to the stack itself.

- **mTCP:** Similar to WATTCP, mTCP offers a modern TCP/IP stack for MS-DOS. However, it caters to a different set of applications and includes additional functionalities like built-in FTP and NTP clients. You can find mTCP bundled with its supported applications within the `WAT2002B.ZIP` package.

- **SSH2DOS:** This software provides MS-DOS versions of essential SSHv2 client applications like SSH, SCP, AND SFTP . These tools enable secure remote login and file transfer capabilities.

- **WGET:** For users unfamiliar with WGET , it's a powerful command-line tool that simplifies the process of downloading files from remote HTTP and FTP servers. This software proves invaluable in environments lacking graphical user interfaces.

- **XFS Network File System Client 1.91:** This software served as a commercial program offering NFS (Network File System) client functionality for MS-DOS. However, due to its discontinued status, downloading the software is readily accessible. **Note:** As XFS Network File System Client 1.91 is no longer actively supported, using it at your own discretion is recommended.

Network Interface Card (NIC) Drivers:

As mentioned earlier, you'll need to acquire drivers specific to your network interface card (NIC) to establish network connectivity for MS-DOS. While the provided compilation includes drivers compatible with my system, it is recommended to locate drivers specific to your own NIC for optimal performance. When selecting drivers, ensure they are compatible with your specific NIC model to avoid potential conflicts and ensure successful network connectivity. If you're unsure about your NIC model, consult your system documentation or utilize system identification tools to determine the correct driver set.

Establishing Network Connectivity:

Now w e embark on the (somewhat) arduous yet ultimately rewarding task of configuring networking. This will significantly minimize the reliance on cumbersome floppy disks, fostering a more streamlined workflow. However, it's important to acknowledge that networking under DOS possesses a certain degree of primitiveness. While achievable, the process necessitates the meticulous installation of various drivers and network protocols, potentially leading to frustration along the way. Nevertheless, with perseverance, we can establish this crucial functionality.

The initial decision revolves around the specific type of networking support desired. In essence, we have the option to install two distinct driver categories:

- **NDIS:** T his modernized driver interface, co-developed by Microsoft, boasts expanded features and capabilities. However, these enhancements come at the cost of increased complexity, potentially introducing bugs and demanding a larger memory footprint. Notably, NDIS is essential for utilizing Microsoft' s networking utilities, including the coveted feature of drive mapping.

- **Packet Driver (PD):** This is t he legacy and open-source driver interface that predates NDIS and enjoys widespread adoption. Most non-Microsoft networking utilities require a PD interface for proper functionality and will simp ly not operate with NDIS alone.

Fortunately, we are not limited to a binary choice. With some additional effort, it is possible to install support for both drivers, providing comprehensive functionality. However, if your needs necessitate only one interface, it's prudent to select the appropriate option to streamline the process.

The ensuing walkthrough will detail the installation of both drivers, highlighting the necessary adjustments if you choose to install only one. It's crucial to remember that the installation sequence varies depending on your desired outcome (PD only, NDIS only, or both).

While PD might initially appear less feature-rich compared to NDIS, it possesses several distinct advantages. Notably, it offers faster setup, increased efficiency, superior reliability, and broader compatibility compared to its newer counterpart. Additionally, a wide range of PD-compatible utilities exist, including DOS versions of SSH, SCP, SFTP, and even an NFS client. These SSH utilities enable secure and effortless file transfer from other systems, eliminating the need for NDIS configuration or Samba support (which typically remains disabled by default). Furthermore, the NFS client allows mounting an NFS share as a DOS drive letter, similar to the functionality of mapped drives.

While NDIS offers a comprehensive experience (and can be conveniently disabled if deemed unnecessary), the PD-only option expedites the setup process. In fact, after extensive experimentation, I have found the PD-only approach to be sufficient for my own system.

With this knowledge in hand, let us proceed confidently and explore the intricacies of network configuration in the realm of DOS.

Configuring Network Interface Cards (NICs) for DOS Networking

Establishing a network connection in your DOS environment requires the installation of appropriate software for your spec ific Network Interface Card (NIC). These cards, also known as NICs, act as the physical connection points between your computer and the network. This section details the steps and resources necessary for configuring three commonly used NICs: the 3Com 3C905C, 3Com 3C509B, and Kingston KNE20T.

Hardware Driver Requirements: Both NDIS (Network Driver Interface Specification) and native Packet Drivers require hardware-specific drivers to function correctly. In my case, I am utilizing a 3Com 3C905C, a Plug and Play (PnP) PCI NIC with a relatively straightforward configuration process. However, if you are using an older ISA (Industry Standard Architecture) NIC, additional steps might be involved, such as specifying the I/O address and interrupt request (IRQ).

Locating and Installing Drivers:

1. Begin by determining the exact model of your NIC. This information can usually be found printed on the card itself or obtained from your computer's documentation.

2. Locate and download the appropriate driver package for your specific NIC. This can often be downloaded from the manufacturer's website or found on installation media accompanying the NIC.

3. Refer to the documentation included with the driver package for detailed installation instructions. These instructions will typically guide you through copying the necessary files and potentially making configuration adjustments.

Specific Instructions for Listed NICs:

The following sections provide details and file requirements for the three NICs mentioned previously:

3Com 3C905C:

`NDIS2\DOS\EL90X.DOS` : NDIS2 driver
`NDIS2\DOS\OEMSETUP.INF` : NDIS2 config file for Microsoft Network Client
`PKTDVR\3C90XPD.COM` : Packet Driver

3Com 3C509B:

`NDIS2\DOS\ELNK3.DOS` : NDIS2 driver
`NDIS2\DOS\OEMSETUP.INF` : NDIS2 config file for Microsoft Network Client
`PKTDVR\3C5X9PD.COM` : Packet Driver
`3C509.COM` : Alternative Crynwr Packet Driver (recommended)

Kingston KNE20T:

NDIS2\KTC20.DOS : NDIS2 driver

NDIS2\LANSERVR.DOS\OEMSETUP.INF : NDIS2 config file

for Microsoft Network Client

PKTDVR\KTC20PKT.COM : Packet Driver

Note: For the Kingston KNE20T, the listed files are in cluded within the pnpdata1.exe file. While it is possible to manually extract these files, using the QStart utility is recommended for a more streamlined process.

Using QStart for Driver Installation (Kingston KNE20T):

1. Run QSTART.EXE :

2. Configure the appropriate Plug and Play mode based on your computer's BIOS capabilities and click Continue.
3. Select Custom from the installation method options.
4. If desired, utilize the Config. options to review your system configuration. Proceed by clicking Continue.
5. Select Basic Test to verify your configuration (optional). Once ready, choose Driver Installation.
6. Select "IBM LAN Server ver. 4.0 DOS LAN Services / NDIS 2" or "Packet Driver" based on your preference. Choose a suitable Destination Directory and click Copy.

7. Select Exit to finalize driver extraction. If you made any configuration changes, especially regarding the PnP mode, restarting your computer is recommended for the changes to take effect.

While this guide provides an overview for these specific NICs, the configuration process might vary slightly depending on the specific model and driver version. Always refer to the accompanying documentation for detailed instructions.

Certain NICs might require additional configuration steps beyond installing drivers, such as setting IRQ and I/O address values. Consult your NIC's documentation for such scenarios.

Installing the Packet Driver (PD Interface Only)

This section outlines the steps for inst alling the Packet Driver (PD) interface, which allows your computer to communicate on a network using a specific network interface card (NIC). This guide assumes you only require the PD interface and do not need additional features provided by the full software suite.

1. Locate the file named `3C90XPD.COM` (or the appropriate driver file for your NIC) and copy it to the `C:\DOS` directory.

2. Open the file `C:\AUTOEXEC.BAT` using a text editor.

3. Locate a blank line or the end of the file and add the following line, ensuring case sensitivity for the /I option:

```
LOADHIGH C:\DOS\3C90XPD.COM /I=0X60
```

4. Save the changes made to the `AUTOEXEC.BAT` .
5. Restart your computer.

Assuming you have an ethernet cable connected, the driver should automatically detect the network connection.

`LOADHIGH C:\DOS\3C90XPD.COM` instructs the computer to load the driver file into high memory for improved performance.

`I=0x60:` This option specifies the software interrupt used by the driver. By default, most cards use 0x60, and changing this value is not recommended unless you have multiple NICs installed.

Note: I f you only require the PD interface for basic network functionality, you can skip to the section titled "Packet Driver Configuration" (if applicable). This guide provides a general overview. Specific instructions and commands might vary depending on your network card model and operating system version. Consult your NIC documentation for details if needed.

Installing Microsoft Network Client 3.0 for MS-DOS (MS-Client)

As you've seen with the previously discussed Peripheral Device (PD) driver, installing an NDIS (Network Driver Interface Specification) driver requires a somewhat different approach. While manual installation is an option, we'll utilize the Microsoft Network Client 3.0 for MS-DOS (MS-Client) software to streamline the process.
MS-Client serves as a multi-protocol stack specifically designed for the MS-DOS environment. This software, however, relies on an NDIS driver to effectively communicate with your network hardware.

Preparation:

1. As recommended earlier, copy both MS-Client disks to your hard drive. Consider creating a backup copy in the `C:\BACKUP` dire ctory as well. This will be the last time we emphasize the importance of creating backups for critical files.

2. Executing each .exe file on the disks will automatically extract the necessary files to your current directory, assuming you haven't done so previously.

3. If prompted, feel free to overwrite any existing files during the extraction process. Some files might be present on both disks if they were copied to a designated directory.

4. Locate the NDIS driver and configuration file specific to your network interface card (NIC) as described earlier. Copy both files to your hard drive, ensuring they reside in the same directory. Make a note of the directory location for future reference.

Special Note for 3c90x Network Cards:

If you're using a network card belonging to the 3C90X series, a slight modification is necessary before proceeding with the MS-Client installation. Open the oemsetup.inf file and comment out or delete the following lines, then save the file after making these changes.

```
NDIS3=1:EL90X.386

MLID=1:3C90X.COM
```

Beginning the Installation:

Once all preparations are complete, navigate to Disk 1 and execute the setup.exe file to initiate the MS-Client installation process.
To configure MS-Client for optimal performance on your system, follow these detailed instructions:

1. Press Enter to skip the welcome screen

```
Setup for Microsoft Network Client v3.0 for MS-DOS

         Welcome to Setup for Microsoft Network Client for MS-DOS.

         Setup prepares Network Client to run on your computer.

         *  To get additional information about a Setup screen,
            press F1.

         *  To set up Network Client now, press ENTER.

         *  To quit Setup without installing Network Client,
            press F3.




ENTER=Continue   F1=Help   F3=Exit   F5=Remove Color
```

2. To begin, navigate to the directory containing the DOS-specific netw ork drivers. Enter `C:\DOS\NET` as the installation directory when prompted by the setup program.

```
Setup for Microsoft Network Client v3.0 for MS-DOS

          Setup will place your Network Client files in
          the following directory.

          If this is where you want these files, press ENTER.

          If you want Setup to place the files in a different
          directory, type the full path of that directory, and
          then press ENTER.


          C:\NET




ENTER=Continue   F1=Help   F3=Exit
```

3. The setup program will list available network adapter drivers. If your hardware is listed, you can select the appropriate driver. However, newer drivers are often available and offer improved performance. Therefore, we recommend choosing "Network adapter not shown on the list below" to utilize your downloaded driver instead.

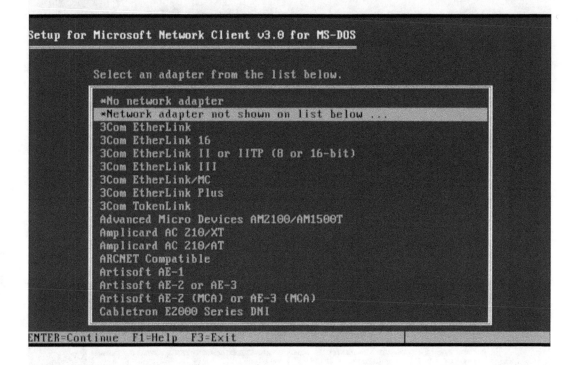

4. The setup program requires the location of your NDIS2 driver configuration file. Enter the exact directory path where this file resides.

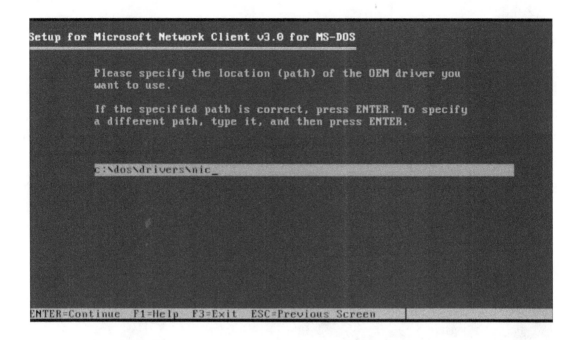

Setup for Microsoft Network Client v3.0 for MS-DOS

Please specify the location (path) of the OEM driver you want to use.

If the specified path is correct, press ENTER. To specify a different path, type it, and then press ENTER.

c:\dos\drivers\nic_

ENTER=Continue   F1=Help   F3=Exit   ESC=Previous Screen

5. Double-check the chosen driver and confirm your selection when prompted.

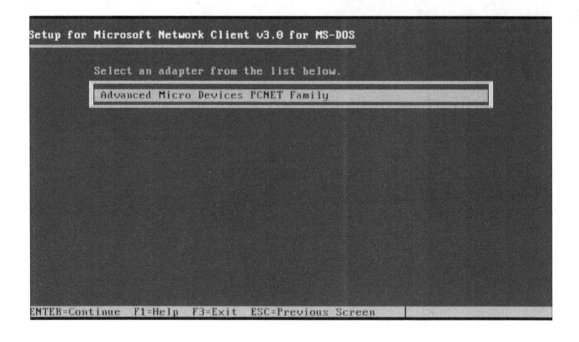

Setup for Microsoft Network Client v3.0 for MS-DOS

Select an adapter from the list below.

Advanced Micro Devices PCNET Family

ENTER=Continue   F1=Help   F3=Exit   ESC=Previous Screen

6. Unless your system is severely limited on RAM, it's recommended to let the Microsoft Network Client optimize itself for performance. Simply press Enter to continue with the default settings.

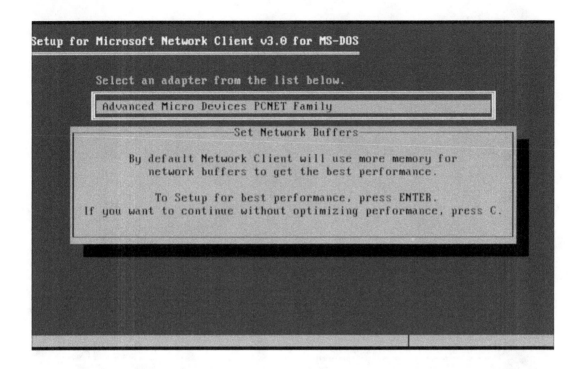

```
Setup for Microsoft Network Client v3.0 for MS-DOS
─────────────────────────────────────────────────

        Select an adapter from the list below.
    ┌─────────────────────────────────────────────┐
    │ Advanced Micro Devices PCNET Family           │
    └─────────────────────────────────────────────┘
    ┌──────────────────Set Network Buffers─────────────────┐
    │                                                       │
    │      By default Network Client will use more memory for│
    │      network buffers to get the best performance.      │
    │                                                       │
    │        To Setup for best performance, press ENTER.    │
    │  If you want to continue without optimizing performance, press C.│
    │                                                       │
    └───────────────────────────────────────────────────────┘
```

7. Provide the username you will use to log in to this computer. This username is
   primarily used for authentication when accessing shared drives on other servers.

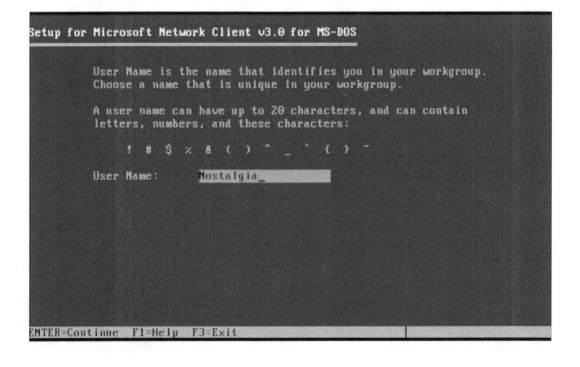

```
Setup for Microsoft Network Client v3.0 for MS-DOS
─────────────────────────────────────────────────

        User Name is the name that identifies you in your workgroup.
        Choose a name that is unique in your workgroup.

        A user name can have up to 20 characters, and can contain
        letters, numbers, and these characters:

            !  #  $  %  &  (  )  ^  _  `  {  }  ~

        User Name:        Nostalgia_


ENTER=Continue  F1=Help  F3=Exit
```

8. After setting the username, choose the "Change Names" option. This allows you to edit your hostname, workgroup, and domain name as necessary for your network configuration.

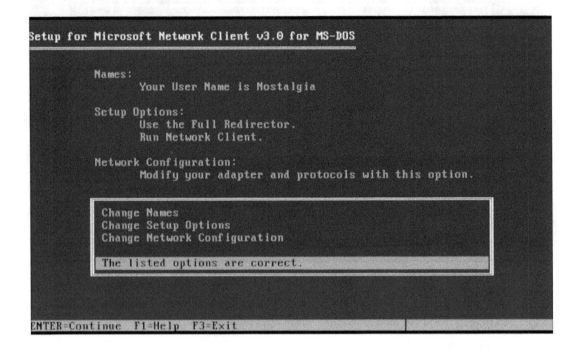

```
Setup for Microsoft Network Client v3.0 for MS-DOS

        Names:
                Your User Name is Nostalgia

        Setup Options:
                Use the Full Redirector.
                Run Network Client.

        Network Configuration:
                Modify your adapter and protocols with this option.

        ┌──────────────────────────────────────────────────────┐
        │ Change Names                                           │
        │ Change Setup Options                                   │
        │ Change Network Configuration                           │
        │                                                        │
        │ The listed options are correct.                        │
        └──────────────────────────────────────────────────────┘


ENTER=Continue   F1=Help   F3=Exit
```

9. Once you have edited the network names, select "The listed names are correct" to return to the main configuration menu.

10. Choose "Change Setup Options" followed by "Change Redir Options". I recommend using the "Basic Redirector" if possible to conserve memory. The "Full Redirector" is only required if you need to authenticate against an NT domain controller.

11. By default, the setup program configures the client to "Run Network Client" automatically at startup. I recommend leaving this option unchanged. The other options are only relevant for specific communication protocols and can be adjusted later if needed.

12. The "Logon Validation" and "Net Pop Hot Key" options are best left at their default settings. You can modify them later if desired. Select "The listed options are correct" to return to the main menu.

13. Choose "Change Network Configuration" to access advanced network settings. This interface can be cumbersome. Use the Tab key to navigate: first select the network adapter/protocol you want to modify, then tab down and choose the appropriate action.

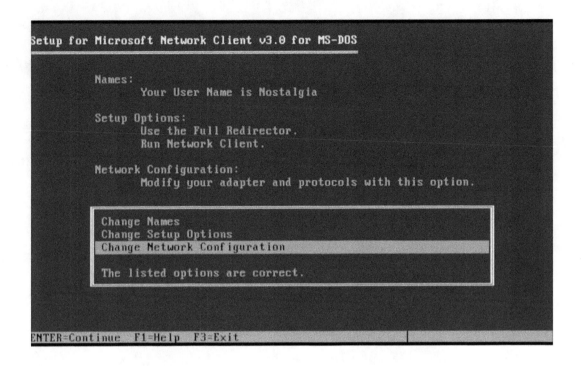

```
    Names:
            Your User Name is Nostalgia

    Setup Options:
            Use the Full Redirector.
            Run Network Client.

    Network Configuration:
            Modify your adapter and protocols with this option.

    ┌──────────────────────────────────────────────────┐
    │  Change Names                                      │
    │  Change Setup Options                              │
    │  Change Network Configuration                      │
    │                                                    │
    │  The listed options are correct.                   │
    └──────────────────────────────────────────────────┘



  ENTER=Continue  F1=Help   F3=Exit
```

14. Begin by selecting your Network Interface Card (NIC) and choosing "Change Settings". Review and update any settings as needed. Generally, you won't need to modify these unless you have multiple NICs. Next, choose "NWLink IPX Compatible Transport" and select "Remove". IPX is an outdated protocol and no longer commonly used.

```
Setup for Microsoft Network Client v3.0 for MS-DOS
━━━━━━━━━━━━━━━━━━━━━━━━━━━━━━━━━━━━━━━━━━━━━━━━━━━━━━

        Use TAB to toggle between boxes.

        Installed Network Adapter(s) and Protocol(s):
      ┌─────────────────────────────────────────────────────┐
      │ Advanced Micro Devices PCNET Family                  │
      │         NWLink IPX Compatible Transport              │
      └─────────────────────────────────────────────────────┘
        Options:
      ┌─────────────────────────────────────────────────────┐
      │ Change Settings                                      │
      │ Remove                                               │
      │ Add Adapter                                          │
      │ Add Protocol                                         │
      │                                                      │
      │ Network configuration is correct.                    │
      └─────────────────────────────────────────────────────┘



ENTER=Continue  F1=Help  F3=Exit
```

15. Following the removal of IPX, choose "Add Protocol" and select "Microsoft TCP/IP". This is the standard protocol used for modern internet communication.

16. Select "Microsoft TCP/IP" and choose "Change Settings". You can configure your IP address and network settings here, but if you're on a network utilizing DHCP (Dynamic Host Configuration Protocol), you can skip this step and return to the Network Configuration menu.

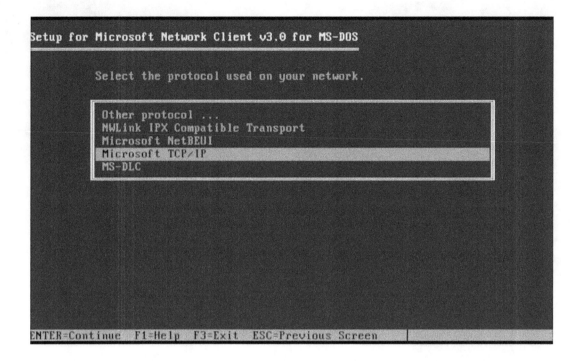

```
Select the protocol used on your network.

    Other protocol ...
    NWLink IPX Compatible Transport
    Microsoft NetBEUI
    Microsoft TCP/IP
    MS-DLC
```

ENTER=Continue   F1=Help   F3=Exit   ESC=Previous Screen

17. If you need to communicate with extremely old DOS or Windows systems (pre-Windows 95), you can optionally install and configure "Microsoft NetBEUI". However, this is generally not necessary as modern server operating systems, including Samba, support NetBIOS over TCP/IP (NBT). NetBEUI itself is not required for NetBIOS communication.

18. Once you've completed configuring the network settings, choose "Network configuration is correct" to return to the main menu.

19. Navigate back to the main configuration menu and choose "The listed options are correct" to proceed with the installation.

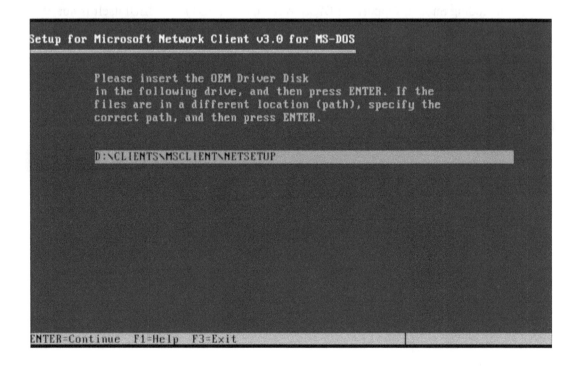

```
Setup for Microsoft Network Client v3.0 for MS-DOS
───────────────────────────────────────────────────

        Names:
                Your User Name is Nostalgia

        Setup Options:
                Use the Full Redirector.
                Run Network Client.

        Network Configuration:
                Modify your adapter and protocols with this option.

        ┌─────────────────────────────────────────────┐
        │ Change Names                                │
        │ Change Setup Options                        │
        │ Change Network Configuration                │
        │                                             │
        │ The listed options are correct.            │
        └─────────────────────────────────────────────┘




ENTER=Continue  F1=Help  F3=Exit
```

20. When prompted for the "OEM Driver Disk", provide the path to "MS-Client Disk
    2". Alternatively, if all files were copied to a single directory, simply press Enter.

```
Setup for Microsoft Network Client v3.0 for MS-DOS
───────────────────────────────────────────────────

        Please insert the OEM Driver Disk
        in the following drive, and then press ENTER. If the
        files are in a different location (path), specify the
        correct path, and then press ENTER.


        D:\CLIENTS\MSCLIENT\NETSETUP








ENTER=Continue  F1=Help  F3=Exit
```

21. Finally, press F3 to exit the setup process without restarting your computer. This allows you to continue with other configuration steps before rebooting the system.

```
Setup for Microsoft Network Client v3.0 for MS-DOS


     Network Client is now installed on your computer.

     Setup modified some settings in your CONFIG.SYS and AUTOEXEC.BAT
     files. Your previous CONFIG.SYS file was saved as C:\CONFIG.001.
     Your previous AUTOEXEC.BAT file was saved as C:\AUTOEXEC.001.

     You must restart your computer before you can use Microsoft
     Network Client for MS-DOS.

     *  To restart your computer, remove all disks from your floppy
        disk drives, and then press ENTER.

     *  To quit Setup without restarting your computer, press F3.




ENTER=Continue   F1=Help   F3=Exit                    |Installation Complete
```

A bug exists within the MS-Client installer, which inadvertently omits a file crucial for Windows 3.1x compatibility. While this file is not strictly required for operating solely within a DOS environment, it safeguards potential future interactions with Windows 3.1x components. Therefore, for comprehensive functionality, I recommend adding this file post installation.

To proceed:

1. Navigate to the directory containing the MS-Client setup files.
2. Within this directory, execute the following command:

```
EXPAND DISK2\WSAHDAPP.EX_
C:\DOS\NET\WSAHDAPP.EXE
```

This command utilizes the EXPAND utility to extract WSAHDAPP.EX_ and renames it to WSAHDAPP.EXE . The file is then placed within the designated directory C:\DOS\NET . Should you encounter additional unforeseen circumstances or require clarification regarding specific installation options, the official MS-Client setup documentation remains accessible through Microsoft's resources.

The MS-Client installation process has modified your system configuration files, namely CONFIG.SYS and AUTOEXEC.BAT . We'll now review these changes and implement a few adjustments to optimize performance.

Config.sys: Locate the line: `DEVICEHIGH=C:\DOS\NET\IFSHLP.SYS` . This line instructs the system to load the Installable File System Helper (IFSHLP) if available. IFSHLP provides crucial file and network access functionalities utilized by MS-Client utilities. We want to load it in high memory by replacing the line with the below

```
DEVICEHIGH=C:\DOS\NET\IFSHLP.SYS
```

Autoexec.bat: locate the following lines: These lines instruct the system to load various network services installed by MS-Client into high memory, enhancing overall system performance. Modify the lines to `LOADHIGH` if they are not already

```
LOADHIGH C:\DOS\NET\TCPTSR.EXE
LOADHIGH C:\DOS\NET\TINYRFC.EXE
LOADHIGH C:\DOS\NET\EMSBFR.EXE
```

Final Step: Once the modifications are complete, reboot your system to ensure the network drivers load successfully.

Note: Please observe that the lines containing `NET *.COM` and `NMTSR.EXE` do not have the `LOADHIGH` prefix. This is essential, as these services require execution from conventional memory to function properly.

If you encounter an error message upon booting, such as "Insufficient memory to load Tiny RFC 1.0" (or similar messages for other services), remove the `LOADHIGH` prefix from the corresponding line. This signifies insufficient upper memory, and attempting to load the service into high memory will fail. MS-Client, unfortunately, lacks the capability to automatically load into conventional memory in such scenarios.

Establishing Network Connectivity: A Step-by-Step Guide

Following the restart process, MS-Client will start on the critical task of initializing your network card. This involves the crucial step of acquiring an IP address, typically achieved through a process known as DHCP (Dynamic Host Configuration Protocol), assuming it's enabled. Once this vital information is secured, the system will prompt you to enter a username.

This username entry is necessary only if you intend to map network drives to your local environment, granting you access to shared resources on other computers. Conversely, if automatic drive mounting upon login isn't your preference, you can simply bypass this step and disable it entirely.

For those seeking to map shared drives, proceed with entering your username (or simply press Enter to accept the choice made during MS-Client setup). Next, provide the password associated with your account to complete the authentication process.

If automatic drive mounting isn't your objective, press Enter twice consecutively. This action creates a NULL password, essentially granting streamlined access without the need for further user authentication.

```
NDIS v2.0.1 MAC Driver, Version 3.12
DriverName ........ PCNTND$
   Station Address ... 08.00.27.2C.A2.F3
Driver configuration.
   IOAddress ........ 0xD020
   Interrupt ........ 9
   DMA .............. 0
   Rx Buffers ..... 4
   Tx Buffers ..... 4
Microsoft DOS TCP/IP Protocol Driver 1.0a
Copyright (c) Microsoft Corporation, 1991.  All rights reserved.
Copyright (c) Hewlett-Packard Corporation, 1985-1991.  All rights reserved.
Copyright (c) 3Com Corporation, 1985-1991.  All rights reserved.
Microsoft DOS TCP/IP NEMM Driver 1.0
The command completed successfully.
MSCDEX Version 2.23
Copyright (C) Microsoft Corp. 1986-1993. All rights reserved.
        Drive D: = Driver CDROM unit 0

CuteMouse v2.0 alpha 4 [FreeDOS]
Installed at PS/2 port
MS-DOS LAN Manager v2.1 Netbind
Initializing TCP/IP via DHCP....
Microsoft DOS TCP/IP 1.0a
Type your user name, or press ENTER if it is NOSTALGIA:_
```

Regardless of your preferred approach, it's strongly recommended to select Y (Yes) when prompted to create a password list. This list serves as a valuable repository of usernames and their corresponding passwords, facilitating convenient login to various network resources.

```
Driver configuration.
   IOAddress ........ 0xD020
   Interrupt ........ 9
   DMA .............. 0
   Rx Buffers ..... 4
   Tx Buffers ..... 4
Microsoft DOS TCP/IP Protocol Driver 1.0a
Copyright (c) Microsoft Corporation, 1991.  All rights reserved.
Copyright (c) Hewlett-Packard Corporation, 1985-1991.  All rights reserved.
Copyright (c) 3Com Corporation, 1985-1991.  All rights reserved.
Microsoft DOS TCP/IP NEMM Driver 1.0
The command completed successfully.
MSCDEX Version 2.23
Copyright (C) Microsoft Corp. 1986-1993. All rights reserved.
        Drive D: = Driver CDROM unit 0

CuteMouse v2.0 alpha 4 [FreeDOS]
Installed at PS/2 port
MS-DOS LAN Manager v2.1 Netbind
Initializing TCP/IP via DHCP....
Microsoft DOS TCP/IP 1.0a
Type your user name, or press ENTER if it is NOSTALGIA:
Type your password:
There is no password-list file for NOSTALGIA.
Do you want to create one? (Y/N) [N]:
```

With these steps completed, Microsoft's TCP/IP stack, the system responsible for network communication, should be largely operational, utilizing the NDIS (Network Driver Interface Specification) driver. While this may seem familiar to users accustomed to modern networking tools, it's crucial to remember that the utilities employed here, although sharing similar names with their contemporary counterparts, operate in a distinctly different manner. As you delve deeper, keep in mind the limitations and "primitive" nature of these early networking tools.

Before embarking on our journey, it's crucial to confirm the establishment of network connectivity between your computer and the outside world.

Checking IP Address:

From the command prompt execute the following command:

```
IPCONFIG C:\DOS\NET
```

This command displays your computer's network configuration, including the all-important IP address. This address is typically assigned automatically by a DHCP server on your network. Alternatively, it may be a static IP address you configured during the MS-Client setup.

Once you have your IP address, utilize the ping command to verify communication with your own computer. At the command prompt, type:

```
PING 192.168.0.15  (Replace with your actual IP address)
```

If the command executes successfully, you should see the message "Reply from 192.168.0.15: bytes=32 time=43ms TTL=64" followed by "Echo reply." This confirms that your computer can successfully communicate with itself, indicating proper network card functionality.

The next step is to verify your computer's ability to communicate with other devices on the network. To achieve this, use the ping command again, but this time, target your gateway's IP address. Typically, this information can be found within the output of the ipconfig command you executed earlier. Look for the line labeled "Default Gateway."

```
PING 10.0.0.1 (Replace with your actual gateway IP address)
```

If successful, you should observe a similar response as in the previous step, indicating successful communication with your network gateway. This signifies that your computer can communicate with other devices beyond itself on the network.

```
Driver configuration.
    IOAddress ......... 0xD020
    Interrupt ......... 9
    DMA .............. 0
    Rx Buffers .....   4
    Tx Buffers .....   4
Microsoft DOS TCP/IP Protocol Driver 1.0a
Copyright (c) Microsoft Corporation, 1991.  All rights reserved.
Copyright (c) Hewlett-Packard Corporation, 1985-1991.  All rights reserved.
Copyright (c) 3Com Corporation, 1985-1991.  All rights reserved.
Microsoft DOS TCP/IP NEMM Driver 1.0
The command completed successfully.
MS-DOS LAN Manager v2.1 Netbind
Initializing TCP/IP via DHCP....
Microsoft DOS TCP/IP 1.0a

Error 2183: The default network services have already been started.

C:\>ping 10.0.0.1
Copyright (c) Microsoft Corporation, 1991-1993.  All rights reserved.
Copyright (c) Hewlett-Packard Corporation, 1985-1993.  All rights reserved.
Copyright (c) 3Com Corporation, 1985-1993.  All rights reserved.
[1] echo received from 10.0.0.1 with roundtrip = 60 msec

C:\>_
```

If all the aforementioned steps yielded the expected responses, congratulations! Your network connection is successfully established, and you can proceed with further configuration.

Addressing DNS Issues:

However, it's vital to address one final hurdle. Due to a known issue with MS-Client, the DNS (Domain Name System) service does not function by default, nor can it be configured through the setup utility. Manual configuration is necessary to enable proper internet browsing and domain resolution.

To enable the Domain Name System (DNS) and allow your MS-DOS system to resolve hostnames on your network, follow these instructions carefully:

1. Locate the file C:\DOS\NET\TCPUTILS.INI   This file holds configuration settings for various network utilities, including the DNS client (DNR).

2. Open the file using a text editor.
3. Navigate to the section labeled [DNR]   (if it doesn't exist, create it).

4. Within the [DNR]   section, add the following lines:

   ```
   DRIVERNAME=DNR$
   BINDINGS=TCPIP_XIF
   ```

5. The line DRIVERNAME=DNR$ identifies the DNS client driver to be used.
6. The line BINDINGS=TCPIP_XIF   specifies that the DNS client should use the TCP/IP driver with the network interface card (XIF) for communication.

Configuring DNS Servers (Optional):

1. If you are not using DHCP to obtain your network settings, add the following lines below the `BINDINGS` line in the `[DNR]` section, replacing the placeholders with your actual network information:

```
NAMESERVER0=AAA BBB CCC DDD


NAMESERVER1=AAA BBB CCC EEE


DOMAIN=DOMAIN.COM
```

The lines `NAMESERVER0` and `NAMESERVER1` specify the IP addresses of your primary and secondary DNS servers, respectively. Replace `AAA BBB CCC DDD` **and** `AAA BBB CCC EEE` with the actual IP addresses of your DNS servers.
The line `DOMAIN=` sets the default domain name to be used when resolving hostnames. Replace `DOMAIN.COM` with your actual domain name.

2. Locate the file `AUTOEXEC.BAT` This file contains commands that are automatically executed when your system starts.

3. Open the file using a text editor.
4. Locate the line `NET START` (usually near the end of the file).

5. Immediately above the line `NET START`, add the following line:

```
LOADHIGH C:\DOS\NET\DNR.EXE
```

6. Save the changes made to both `TCPUTILS.INI` and `AUTOEXEC.BAT`
7. Restart your computer for the changes to take effect.

The `LOADHIGH` command instructs the system to load the DNR executable file into high memory, improving performance. The path `C:\DOS\NET\DNR.EXE` specifies the location of the DNS client executable file.
Note: Ensure you replace the placeholders (`AAA BBB CCC DDD`, `AAA BBB CCC EEE`, and `DOMAIN.COM`) with your actual network information. Separate the octets in the IP addresses with spaces, unlike the dot notation used in modern systems. This guide assumes you are using the built-in TCP/IP stack. If you're using a different networking stack, the configuration steps might differ.

Domain Resolution and Shared Resources

Having established network connectivity, we now turn our attention to resolving domain names and accessing shared network resources. This crucial step paves the way for seamless file transfer and software installation, eliminating the reliance on cumbersome floppy disks.

Activating the Microsoft Domain Name Resolver:

To translate user-friendly domain names like " www.google.com " into their corresponding numerical IP addresses, we utilize the Microsoft Domain Name Resolver (DNS). Execute the following command from the command prompt:

```
NET START DNSCLIENT
```

This command initiates the DNS client service, enabling your system to interact with DNS servers and translate domain names effectively.

Verifying DNS Functionality:

Once activated, we can verify the functionality of the DNS client by retrying the previously used ping command, this time directed at a website:

```
PING  www.google.com
```

Assuming successful resolution, you should receive a familiar response with the message "Reply from x.x.x.x: bytes=32 time=xxxms TTL=xx" (where "x" represents the received data and response time). This confirms that your system can successfully utilize DNS to translate domain names into their corresponding IP addresses.

Unveiling the Power of Shared Network Drives:

By harnessing the power of your network, you can now access shared network drives. These drives reside on other computers on the network and can be accessed by authorized users, enabling efficient file sharing and application installation.

This capability revolutionizes the way you interact with your network, offering a convenient and centralized location for managing data and software. Imagine the ease of installing a new application or copying a large file simply by accessing a shared drive, eliminating the need for multiple floppy disks and the associated time-consuming transfers. This section outlines the process for mapping a network drive on systems predating modern graphical user interfaces (GUIs). Please note that configuring the shared drive on the server (e.g., Samba or Windows server) is beyond the scope of this guide.

Assuming you have already configured a shared drive on a remote server, you can proceed with mapping the drive locally using the following command:

```
NET USE E: \\SERVERNAME\SHARENAME
```

Replace E: with your desired drive letter and \\SERVERNAME\SHARENAME with the actual server name and shared folder name.

Assuming the server is properly configured and your credentials are valid, this command should execute successfully, and you will receive a "command completed successfully" message.

To verify the connection, use the DIR E: command. If the command successfully displays the contents of the shared folder, the mapping has been established.

However, it is crucial to note that modern versions of Samba and Windows servers may not support DOS or Windows 3.x clients by default. To enable this functionality, modifications on the server-side might be required, potentially introducing security vulnerabilities. This guide cannot provide specific instructions due to the security implications and the variations in server configurations.

If you encounter difficulties with network drive mapping, alternative methods like SCP, SFTP, and NFS offer more reliable and secure options for file transfer using the provided PD interface. These methods will be explained in detail in subsequent sections.

This guide emphasizes that while mapping network drives can be achieved on older systems, it is important to be aware of the potential security risks and limitations associated with using outdated protocols on modern servers. Alternative methods, as outlined later in the guide, are generally recommended for secure and reliable file transfer.

To further empower your MS-DOS system's networking capabilities, we'll delve into the installation and configuration of an NDIS Packet Driver Shim. This ingenious tool acts as a bridge, seamlessly merging the functionality of Microsoft's native networking utilities (including those for mapped drives) with the broader realm of non-Microsoft network applications, significantly enriching your networking experience.

Understanding the Shim's Role:

Imagine the NDIS driver as a specialized interpreter, capable of translating the high-level commands issued by your operating system into instructions readily understood by your network interface card (NIC). While this driver excels in its core function, it can present limitations when attempting to utilize a diverse range of network utilities beyond Microsoft's offerings.

Enter the NDIS Packet Driver Shim. This ingenious software component bridges the gap, effectively adding a "PD interface" (packet driver interface) to the existing NDIS driver. With this interface in place, your system gains the remarkable ability to seamlessly interact with a wider spectrum of network tools, empowering you to leverage the full potential of your network.

Important Caveats:

It's crucial to remember that the NDIS Packet Driver Shim serves a specific purpose. While it acts as a bridge between NDIS drivers and various network utilities, it cannot function as a standalone driver for your NIC. The NDIS driver remains an essential component, and the shim cannot directly interact with your NIC without its presence. Additionally, while the shim itself delivers exceptional performance, it's vital to acknowledge the underlying methodology. The very concept of the shim represents a "hack," a workaround that deviates from standard protocols. Consequently, the setup process necessitates manual intervention and might seem intricate to some users.

Installation and Configuration:

1. Begin by copying the file named " DIS_PKT.DOS " to the designated directory: C:\DOS\NET
2. Navigate to the file " PROTOCOL.INI " located within the C:\DOS\NET directory and edit its contents. Append the following lines, ensuring precise accuracy:

```
[PKTDRV]
DRIVERNAME=PKTDRV$
```

```
BINDINGS=TCM$EL90X
INTVEC=0X60
CHAINVEC=0X68
```

3. Locate the `[TCPIP]` section within the `PROTOCOL.INI` file. This section typically contains a line labeled `BINDINGS`.

4. The value associated with the `BINDINGS` line specifies the NDIS driver to which the packet driver needs to bind.

5. Crucially, the value of the `BINDINGS` line for the `[PKTDRV]` section should mirror the corresponding value found in the `[ TCPIP ]` section. This ensures proper communication between the packet driver and the NDIS driver.

6. Open the `CONFIG.SYS` file, which manages device driver loading during system startup.

7. Following the line containing `IFSHLP.SYS`, add the following lines individually:

```
DEVICEHIGH=C:\DOS\NET\PROTMAN.DOS
/I:C:\DOS\NET
DEVICEHIGH=C:\DOS\NET\NEMM.DOS
DEVICEHIGH=C:\DOS\NET\TCPDRV.DOS
DEVICEHIGH=C:\DOS\NET\EL90X.DOS
```

8. While this may appear like a significant addition, you're essentially loading a single new driver: `DIS_PKT.DOS`.

9. The other listed drivers were previously loaded automatically by MS-Client. However, a specific dependency order is crucial for proper operation. This revised configuration ensures that the necessary drivers are loaded in the correct sequence, allowing `DIS_PKT.DOS` to function effectively before MS-Client itself is loaded.

10. Save the modifications made to both `PROTOCOL.INI` and `CONFIG.SYS`.

11. Restart your computer for the changes to take effect.

NDIS Driver Configuration:

The line `EL90X.DOS` within your `CONFIG.SYS` file references the Network Driver Interface Specification (NDIS) driver specific to your 3Com 3C905C network card. It's crucial to replace this entry with the appropriate NDIS driver designated for your own network hardware. Ensure you acquire the correct driver from your network card's manufacturer or a trustworthy source.

Following the successful configuration of `CONFIG.SYS`, we turn our attention to editing the `AUTOEXEC.BAT` file. Here, we address two key adjustments.

The comman d `REM C:\DOS\NET\NET INITIALIZE` is no longer necessary. Previously, it served the purpose of initializing drivers pertinent to MS-Client. However, with the manual loading of drivers through `CONFIG.SYS`, this command becomes redundant and can even lead to errors if executed alongside the already loaded drivers. Comment out this line using the rem prefix to render it inactive.

The line rem `C:\DOS\NET\NET START` enables the automatic mapping of shared network drives upon system boot. If you don't intend to utilize sha red drives, or prefer manual mapping through the net start command whenever needed, comment out this line as well. This action helps conserve a notable amount of conventional memory, which can be beneficial for older systems.

Once these modifications are complete, restart your system to implement the changes. During the boot process, you should observe a message confirming the successful loading of the shim driver, typically resembling: "MAC/DIS to Packet Driver convert loaded." This confirmation signifies that your network adapter is now properly configured and ready for operation.

While we have successfully installed the appropriate packet driver (PD) for your network card, it's important to understand that this is just the first step. Unlike modern operating systems, these drivers merely provide an interface for your network card and don't offer built-in network functionality like TCP/IP communication, IP address assignment, or other essential services.

Each application that utilizes the Packet Driver requires its own network stack to handle these tasks. Traditionally, the Waterloo TCP/IP stack (WATTCP) played a prominent role. This compact and versatile stack could be directly integrated into applications, providing all the necessary network functionalities.

However, advancements have brought us a more modern alternative—the mTCP stack. Offering similar functionalities to WATTCP, mTCP boasts additional utilities that weren't readily available with its predecessor.

Fortunately, both WATTCP and mTCP can coexist and function simultaneously within your system. This allows us to leverage the strengths of both, ensuring compatibility with a wider range of classic applications. In the following steps, we will guide you through the setup and configuration of both network stacks.

Configuring the WATTCP Network Stack

To establish a network connection using WATTCP, we must first configure it with the necessary details. This process involves creating a configuration file and updating your system's startup script.

Creating the Configuration File:

1. Navigate to the directory where WATTCP is installed. This is typically `C:\APPS` by default.

2. Using a text editor, create a new file named `WATTCP.CFG`.

3. Within the file, insert the following lines, replacing `<hostname>` with your desire d computer name:

```
PRINT = "CONFIGURING WATTCP..."
HOSTNAME = <HOSTNAME>
MY_IP = DHCP
```

Setting Static IP Address (Optional):

If you are not using a DHCP server for automatic IP assignment, you will need to configure WATTCP with a static IP address. First, Remove th e line `MY_IP = DHCP` from the conf iguration file. Then Add the following lines, replacing the values with your desired network settings:

```
DOMAIN.SUFFIX = LOCALDOMAIN
MY_IP = 0.0.0.0
NETMASK = 255.255.255.0
NAMESERVER = 0.0.0.0
NAMESERVER = 0.0.0.0
GATEWAY = 0.0.0.0
```

Replace the placeholders with your specific IP address, subnet mask, primary and secondary DNS servers, and default gateway address.

Saving and Integrating Configuration:

1. Save the changes made to the `WATTCP.CFG` file.

2. Open the `AUTOEXEC.BAT` File

3. Add the following line replacing the path if needed:

```
SET WATTCP.CFG=C:\APPS
```

Note: This line sets an environment variable pointing to the location of the configuration file.

4. Save the changes made to the `AUTOEXEC.BAT` File

5. Restart your computer for the changes to take effect.

6. At the command prompt execute the following command:

```
TCPINFO.EXE
```

7. The output should display "Reading Waterloo TCP configuration file," indicating the successful loading of the configuration. Additionally, the displayed network parameters should match your settings or reflect the DHCP assignment.
8. At the command prompt, execute the following command, replacing `www.google.com` with the desired website:

```
PINGW www.google.com
```

If the response displays "Replies lost: 0," congratulations! Your WATTCP configuration is successful, and you are connected to the network.

Note: To avoid conflicts with potentially existing versions of `PING.EXE`, it is recommended to rename the WATTCP version to `PINGW.EXE` as suggested in the original guide.

Configuring mTCP for Network Access

mTCP, like its counterpart WATTCP, facilitates network connectivity for your MS-DOS system. The configuration process involves creating a configuration file and updating your `AUTOEXEC.BAT` file.

mTCP Configuration File:

1. Create a new text file named `mTCP.CFG` in the directory `C:\APPS`.

2. Within this file, add the following lines, replacing `<HOSTNAME>` with your desired machine name:

```
PACKETINT 0X60
HOSTNAME <HOSTNAME>
```

3. If you intend to use a static IP address instead of DHCP, you must add additional lines with appropriate values:

```
IPADDR 0.0.0.0 (REPLACE WITH YOUR IP ADDRESS)
NETMASK 255.255.255.0 (SUBNET MASK)
GATEWAY 0.0.0.0 (DEFAULT GATEWAY)
NAMESERVER 0.0.0.0 (DNS SERVER)
MTU 1500 (MAXIMUM TRANSMISSION UNIT)
```

4. Save and close the file.

Autoexec.bat Edits:

1. Open your `AUTOEXEC.BAT` file, located in the root directory of your C drive
2. Add the following line at the end of the file:

```
SET MTCPCFG=C:\APPS\MTCP.CFG
```

3. If you are using a static IP address (configured in `mTCP.CFG`), you can skip the next step.
4. Add another line below the previous one:

```
C:\APPS\DHCP.EXE
```

5. Save the `AUTOEXEC.BAT` file.

6. To verify successful configuration, copy the `PING.EXE` application to your `C:\APPS` directory. It is recommended to rename it (e.g., `PINGM.EXE`) to avoid conflicts with any existing system files.

7. At the command prompt and execute the following command:

```
PINGM www.google.com
```

If you see a message like "Success: 100%", congratulations! Your mTCP configuration is functional, and your system can access the internet.

Essential Network Tools for Your DOS System

In this section, we will explore the installation and configuration of some essential network applications that can enhance your DOS experience. While numerous options exist, we will focus on those offering significant utility.

Secure Shell (SSH):

For individuals primarily working with Linux systems, Secure Shell (SSH) becomes an invaluable tool. It provides a secure and encrypted channel for remote login and command execution, safeguarding your data and access. Additionally, SSH offers the following benefits:

- **SCP (Secure Copy):** This utility enables the secure transfer of files between your DOS system and remote hosts, offering an alternative to potentially unreliable solutions like NDIS/MS-Client or mapped drives, especially when dealing with modern Samba or Windows servers.

- **SFTP (SSH File Transfer Protocol):** Similar to SCP, SFTP allows for secure file transfer, often integrated within SSH clients for seamless file management.

Fortunately, we have access to an exceptional SSHv2 implementation for DOS, aptly named SSH2DOS. This application can be downloaded from https://sshdos.sourceforge.net/ .

Installing SSH2DOS:

To install SSH2DOS Copy the downloaded files and rename them as follows:

```
SCP2D386.EXE   C:\APPS\SCP.EXE
SFTPD386.EXE   C:\APPS\SFTP.EXE
SSH2D386.EXE   C:\APPS\SSH.EXE
```

System Requirements:

SSH2DOS is based on the WATTCP library, necessitating two crucial elements for successful operation. The Packet Driver Interface which is a software component that allows your DOS system to interact with your network card, enabling network communication and a Functional WATTCP.CFG File. This configuration file defines various network parameters for WATTCP applications. If you have already configured these elements as outlined earlier, you can proceed to the next step.

Verifying Functionality:

To verify the successful installation and functionality of SSH, at the command prompt type the following command, replacing USERNAME with your actual username and SERVERNAME   with the hostname or IP address of the remote server you wish to connect to:

```
SSH USERNAME SERVERNAME
```

If the command prompts you for your password and establishes a secure connection, you have successfully set up SSH2DOS.

Note: SSH2DOS includes a well-commented example WATTCP.CFG file. If you encounter any difficulties with your WATTCP applications or want to explore available configuration options, examining this file can provide valuable insights.

Modifying Configuration:

Should you choose to modify and utilize the provided example configuration file, you have two options. Overwrite the existing WATTCP.CFG file located in C:\DOS or modify the WATTTCP.CFG variable within your AUTOEXEC.BAT file to point to the new location of the configuration file. Remember to update the variable accordingly or reboot your system to ensure applications use the updated configuration.

WGET

WGET , a powerful command-line tool, stands as another valuable addition to your DOS toolkit. Its primary function lies in downloading files from a diverse range of web and FTP servers. While the DOS version, accessible through the provided link, is no longer actively maintained, it remains functional for its intended purpose.

Installation, similar to SSH2DOS, is a straightforward process. Simply copy the `WGET.EXE` file located within the `BIN` directory to your designated application folder, typically `C:\APPS`. As a WATTCP-based application, `WGET` should function seamlessly within your existing DOS environment.

Key benefits of employing WGET include:

Efficiency: `WGET` streamlines the download process, eliminating the need for repetitive manual steps.

Versatility: It possesses the ability to download files from a wide array of online sources, providing flexibility for various use cases.

Command-line control: For users comfortable with the command line, `WGET` offers a familiar and efficient interface for managing downloads.

While the DOS version of `WGET` may not receive ongoing updates, it remains a reliable tool for downloading files within a DOS environment. This is particularly pertinent for those seeking to explore and utilize older software or systems that lack more modern download functionalities.

Installing and Utilizing mTCP Applications

As we proceed with configuring mTCP, let's delve into the installation and practical applications of three valuable utilities included within the distribution: FTP, Telnet, and SNTP.

These utilities are conveniently bundled with the mTCP distribution, eliminating the need for separate acquisition. To install them, simply copy the following files from the mTCP directory to your designated application folder, typically located at `C:\APPS`:

```
FTP.EXE
SNTP.EXE
TELNET.EXE
```

Utilizing Existing Configuration:

Fortunately, these applications leverage the existing mTCP configuration file, allowing you to use them immediately without further configuration steps.

FTP (File Transfer Protocol): For those accustomed to Windows environments on their primary machines, FTP provides a familiar and convenient solution in the absence of SSH. It facilitates the transfer of files between your computer and remote servers.

Telnet (TELecommunication NETwork): This application offers a text-based interface for remote access to other networked devices. It allows you to interact with the target system's command line as if you were physically present.

SNTP (Simple Network Time Protocol): This versatile utility, arguably the most interesting of the three, synchronizes your computer's clock with a reliable NTP server, ensuring accurate timekeeping. This is particularly beneficial for older machines prone to unreliable CMOS batteries.

Setting the Time Zone and Testing SNTP:

Execute the following command from the command prompt. This sets the time zone to Central Standard Time (CST). Consult the accompanying `sntp.txt` file for instructions on adjusting this parameter for other time zones.

```
SET TZ=CST6CDT
```

To test the functionality, run. This command retrieves the current time from the NTP server and displays both your system time and the server's time.

```
SNTP.EXE POOL.NTP.ORG
```

To permanently synchronize your system clock with the NTP server, execute the following command:

```
SNTP.EXE -SET POOL.NTP.ORG
```

For seamless timekeeping on every boot, add the following line (with `-SET`) to your `AUTOEXEC.BAT` file:

```
SNTP.EXE -SET POOL.NTP.ORG
```

Mounting Network Files with XFS (NFS Client) for DOS :

While these three utilities represent my personal favorites, both WATTCP and mTCP offer an array of additional applications and utilities waiting to be discovered. Feel free to explore them and discover tools that may suit your specific needs.

This section explores the possibility of accessing remote file systems using the Network File System (NFS) protocol within a DOS environment. While alternative options like SMB/CIFS servers exist, NFS offers a different approach.

The Good News: You can mount an NFS share directly from DOS using the XFS Network File System Client. XFS acts as an NFS client, allowing your DOS system to interact with NFS servers.

The Not-So-Good News: XFS utilizes its own network driver that conflicts with most other packet driver -based applications. This means simultaneously running XFS and other PD applications like `WGET` or network utilities built on WATTCP or mTCP libraries might not be feasible. If you primarily rely on NDIS-based applications (drivers designed for the Network Driver Interface Specification), XFS shouldn't cause any issues.

Navigating Compatibility Challenges: Theoretically, Packet Driver applications can be configured to work alongside XFS by changing their interrupt vector settings. However, this process might not be straightforward and may require further research and experimentation. If you require both NDIS and PD applications, using NFS with XFS might not be the ideal solution at this time. Consider alternative approaches or choosing between NDIS and PD-based applications.

Getting Started with XFS:

1. Obtain a copy of XFS Network File System Client, which is no longer commercially supported.

2. Review the `KERNELS.TXT` file within the XFS package. This file details the various available kernel drivers. Choose the one that best suits your memory constraints and functionality needs. Common options include the minimal kernel `XFSKRNLM`.

3. Proceed with the installation and configuration of XFS as per the provided instructions.

Additional Considerations: While XFS is an option for accessing NFS shares in DOS, it's important to be aware of its limitations and potential compatibility challenges. Alternative solutions might be more suitable depending on your specific needs and the software you intend to use.

Configuring the XFS Network File System Client for MS-DOS

The following steps outline the installation and configuration process for the XFS Network File System (NFS) client on your MS-DOS system. Please note that this process requires a moderate understanding of MS-DOS configuration and networking concepts.

File Transfer and Organization:

Transfer the following files to the `C:\APPS` directory on your MS-DOS system. It's recommended to rename `LS.EXE` to `LSX.EXE` to avoid potential conflicts with existing aliases or commands in your MS-DOS environment.

```
XFSKRNLM.EXE
HOSTS
LS.EXE
XFSTOOL.EXE
```

Host File Configuration:

1. Open the `HOSTS` file located in the root directory (`C:\`) in a text editor

2. Comment out all existing entries in the file using a ; symbol at the beginning of each line.

3. Add a new line defining your NFS server, following this format:

```
AAA.BBB.CCC.DDD          NFSSERVER.DOMAIN.COM
        NFSSERVER
```

Replace the placeholders with the actual IP address of your NFS server, its domain name (optional), and a chosen alias (`NFSSERVER` in this example).

Static IP Configuration (Optional):

If your MS-DOS system uses a static IP address, add the following lines to the hosts file, replacing the placeholders with your specific network configuration:

```
AAA.BBB.CCC.EEE          GATEWAY
AAA.BBB.CCC.GGG NETMASK
AAA.BBB.CCC.FFF          BROADCAST
AAA.BBB.CCC.GGG          NFSCLIENT.DOMAIN.COM
          NFSCLIENT
```

Replace:

AAA.BBB.CCC.EEE with your network gateway address.
AAA.BBB.CCC.GGG with your subnet mask.
AAA.BBB.CCC.FFF with your network broadcast address.
NFSCLIENT.DOMAIN.COM with your chosen alias for your MS-DOS system
(optional).

NDIS Driver Configuration (Optional):

If you're using NDIS (Network Driver Interface Specification) for networking, follow these additional steps:

1. Copy the file DIS_PKT9.TCP to the C:\DOS\NET directory.

2. Open the CONFIG.SYS file located in the root directory (C:\ ).
3. Locate the line DEVICEHIGH=C:\DOS\NET\DIS_PKT.DOS (if present) and comment it out using a ; symbol at the beginning of the line.

4. Add a new line with the following command:

```
DEVICEHIGH=C:\DOS\NET\DIS_PKT9.TCP
```

This replaces the old packet driver with the one provided by XFS. Reboot your system after completing this step.

5. At the command prompt and execute the following command to initialize the XFS kernel module:

```
LOADHIGH C:\APPS\XFSKRNLM.EXE 0X60
```

6. Next, initialize the XFS driver using the appropriate command based on your network configuration:

For BOOTP (Boot Protocol):
```
XFSTOOL INIT BOOTP
```
For Static IP Address:
```
XFSTOOL INIT NFSCLIENT
```

Replace NFSCLIENT with the alias you defined for your MS-DOS system in step 3 (if applicable).

7. Finally, attempt to mount a shared directory from your NFS server using the following command:

```
XFSTOOL MOUNT F: NFSSERVER:/HOME/DATA/FILES
```

Replace:
`F:` with the desired drive letter for the mounted share.
`NFSSERVER` with the alias you assigned to your NFS server in step 2.
`/HOME/DATA/FILES` with the actual path to the shared directory on your NFS server.
If successful, you should be able to access files and folders within the mounted share using the assigned drive letter (e.g ., `F:\`).

Hostname Configuration:

The X File System (XFS) software requires your system to have a designated local hostname. This hostname serves as an identifier for your computer within the network. If you've opted for a static IP address, the hostname configuration should already be established.
However, if you're employing the BOOTP (Bootstrap Protocol) protocol for dynamic IP assignment, your DHCP (Dynamic Host Configuration Protocol) server plays a crucial role. It must be configured to furnish your system with both an IP address and a corresponding hostname simultaneously. Should you encounter error messages from XFSTOOL regarding an absent hostname, this situation is likely the culprit.
The most straightforward solution in this scenario is to switch to a static IP address for XFS, adhering to the instructions outlined previously.
Once you've successfully configured XFS, executing the command `DIR F:` should display a directory listing of the files present on your NFS server. To access this remote directory, simply switch to the assigned drive letter (`F:` in this example) and utilize the command `LS` (or `LSX`) to view the filenames in a more detailed format.
In instances where the Network Driver Interface Specification (NDIS) protocol is employed, it's advisable to conduct a test of an NDIS application. This serves to verify the proper functioning of the shim driver. A simple test can be performed by utilizing the `PING` command, followed by the assigned hostname (`PING HOSTNAME`). For a more comprehensive assessment, consider mapping a shared drive, for instance, using the command `NET START` .

Automating NFS Mounts:

To establish the automatic mounting of NFS shares upon system startup, incorporate the three commands mentioned earlier (XFSKRNL, INIT, and MOUNT) into your `AUTOEXEC.BAT` file. It's crucial to ensure these commands are positioned after any other network-related applications, such as the mTCP DHCP client, within the `AUTOEXEC.BAT` file. Failure to do so might result in malfunctions of those applications, as mentioned previously.

While XFS's inherent design precludes seamless integration with other PD applications, it offers a unique workaround through its ability to temporarily unload and reload its PD shim. This functionality allows you to switch between XFS and other PD applications without compromising NFS support or necessitating a system reboot.

Imagine a scenario where you have an NFS share mounted and desire to utilize SSH for remote access to another system. By employing XFS's PD shim unloading feature, you can achieve this seamlessly. Briefly halting the PD shim using the `XFSTOOL PKTDRV STOP` command temporarily renders your mounted NFS share inaccessible, paving the way for you to utilize SSH through the command `SSH USERNAME HOSTNAME`. Once finished with SSH, executing the `XFSTOOL PKTDRV RESTART` command reactivates the PD shim, restoring access to your mounted NFS share.

While not an ideal solution, this approach presents a viable compromise. To further streamline this process, consider creating a 4DOS alias (as detailed in the dedicated section) that simplifies the command sequence, minimizing repetitive actions and enhancing user experience.

Configuring Device Drivers and Applications

Software and Drivers:

With the network connection established, transferring files to and from your DOS system has become significantly easier. Now, let's turn our attention to installing the remaining essential drivers and applications. We'll begin by configuring the CD-ROM drive.

Installing a CD-ROM Driver for MS-DOS

MS-DOS itself does not inherently possess the capability to interact with CD-ROM drives. Fortunately, generic drivers exist that act as intermediaries, enabling MS-DOS to communicate with these devices. While obtaining manufacturer-specific drivers might be challenging nowadays, several open-source and widely-compatible options are readily available.

Popular choices include drivers from Oak Technologies and the Adaptec ASPI CD-ROM Driver, both readily downloadable from online repositories. The below table lists alternative MS-DOS CD-ROM drivers

`ASPICD.SYS`	Adaptec ASPI CD-ROM Driver (Supports Yamaha, Kodak, HP C4324/c4325, Plextor, Shinaken, Matshita, DEC, IBM, Teac, Compaq, Chinon, Denon, Hitachi, LMS, NEC, Panasonic, Sony, Toshiba, Texel, JVC, IMS and Pioneer brands).
`BTCDROM.SYS`	CDROM Driver for Buslogic Controller Cards (Supports Sony, Toshiba, Chinon, Hitachi, Texel, Matshita, NEC, IBM, Shinaken, Pioneer, Plextor, Sanyo, Teac, and Aiwa Brands).
`ATAPICD.SYS`	Standard ATAPI CD/DVD-ROM Device Driver v2.12
`GCDROM.SYS`	SATA Native IDE CD/DVD-ROM driver (Supports Intel ICH6/ICH7/ICH8, JMicron 361/363/368, NVidia CK804/MCP55/MCP51...(may not work with PATA)
`OAKCDROM.SYS`	Oak Technologies universal IDE CD-ROM device driver. This driver works with the majority of CD-ROM and DVD-ROM/DVD-R drives made during the DOS era.
`QCDROM.SYS`	UltraDMA CDROM Driver (Supports ATAPI-standard CD/DVD Drives attached to normal PC system IDE channels)
`SBIDE.SYS`	Creative OTI-011 CD-ROM device driver (Marvell PATA Driver).
`SHSUCDX.EXE`	A replacement for the DOS MSCDEX.EXE program. Can be used to provide CD-ROM access when using DOSLFN for long filename support under pure DOS.
`SHSUCD`	The full suite of tools including SHSUCDX, including the ability the create an image file from a CD, simulate a CD-ROM from an image file, a CD-ROM tester, and a replacement for SMARTDRV that works with SHSUCDX.
`Sony 55e`	Sony 55e CD-ROM Driver (IDE) v2.00
`USBCD1.SYS`	Panasonic USB CD-ROM Device Driver 1.0
`USBCD2.SYS`	TEAC USB CD-ROM Device Driver.

Installation Steps:

1. Obtain your driver of choice from a reputable online source.

2. Transfer the downloaded file to the `C:\DOS` directory on your MS-DOS system.

3. Using a text editor, open the CONFIG.SYS file located in the root directory of your boot drive (typically C:).

4. Within the CONFIG.SYS file, add the following line, replacing X with your desired drive letter (commonly D) and CDROMDRV.SYS with the file name of the driver you chose:

```
DEVICEHIGH=C:\DOS\[CDROMDRV.SYS] /D:X
```

5. Open the AUTOEXEC.BAT file, also located in the root directory of your boot drive.
6. Within the autoexec.bat file, add the following line, replacing X with the same drive letter used in step 4:

```
LOADHIGH C:\DOS\MSCDEX.EXE /D:X
```

Explanation:

The DEVICEHIGH command instructs MS-DOS to load the CD-ROM driver in high memory, minimizing its impact on available conventional memory.

The /D option within both lines specifies the drive letter to be associated with the CD-ROM drive.

The MSCDEX.EXE program acts as a translator, enabling communication between MS-DOS and the CD-ROM driver.

Verification:

1. Restart your MS-DOS system for the changes to take effect.

2. During the boot process, you should observe a message similar to:

```
Drive X: = Driver MSCD001 unit 0
```

3. Insert a CD-ROM and execute the DIR [X:] command to confirm that MS-DOS can successfully access the drive contents.

By following these steps and utilizing the recommended driver, you can effectively equip your MS-DOS system with the necessary capabilities to interact with CD-ROM drives, expanding its functionality and allowing you to utilize a broader range of software and resources.

Installing a Mouse Driver for Enhanced Interaction (Optional)

While MS-DOS itself doesn't require a mouse driver, many applications, such as text editors and games, benefit from their functionality. Therefore, installing a mouse driver enhances the user experience by enabling smoother and more intuitive interaction with these programs.

Similar to CD-ROM support, MS-DOS lacks a built-in mouse driver. However, two viable options exist for users seeking to incorporate mouse functionality:

- **Microsoft Mouse Driver** (`MOUSE.COM`): This driver, provided with the Windows 3.x operating system, is available for download from the Computer Hope hardware downloads page.

- **CuteMouse:** This open-source driver, actively developed for the FreeDOS project, offers broader support for modern mouse features like scroll wheels (though application support for these features might vary). Additionally, CuteMouse boasts a significantly smaller memory footprint compared to `MOUSE.COM` (3.5 KB versus 18 KB).

Due to its compact size and active development, CuteMouse is the recommended choice in this instance. However, the choice ultimately rests with the user's preference.

Installation Steps for CuteMouse:

1. Locate the downloaded file, typically named " `CTMOUSE.EXE` ," and copy it to the `C:\DOS` directory.

2. Open the `AUTOEXEC.BAT` file, located in the root directory of your C drive (usually `C:\`).

3. Within the `AUTOEXEC.BAT` file, add the following line, replacing `/3` with the desired options if necessary (consult the CuteMouse documentation for available options):

```
C:\DOS\CTMOUSE.EXE /3
```

4. Save the changes made to `AUTOEXEC.BAT` The `/3` option in the example forces the driver to operate in 3-button mode, a feature not enabled by default.
5. To manually load the driver, At the command prompt and type the command:

```
C:\DOS\CTMOUSE.EXE
```

6. Launch a mouse-compatible application, such as Pedit (text editor) or the included `MOUSETST.COM` utility, to test if the mouse is detected and functional.

Note: CuteMouse is designed to automatically load into upper memory when available, eliminating the need for the `LOADHIGH` command commonly used with older drivers.

Installing Sound Card Drivers for MS-DOS

The first step in enabling sound functionality within your MS-DOS environment involves procuring the appropriate drivers for your sound card. These drivers act as essential intermediaries, allowing your operating system to communicate effectively with the hardware and translate commands into audible output.

In this example, we will demonstrate th e installation process for a Creative Labs Sound Blaster AWE64. While your specific hardware might differ, the general principles remain consistent. It's crucial to obtain drivers compatible with your unique sound card model.

Installation:

1. Ensure you have obtained the driver files for your specific sound card. These might be available online, on physical disks provided with the hardware, or downloaded from the manufacturer's website.

2. Extract the downloaded files or copy the contents of the driver disk to an accessible location on your hard drive. Typically, creating a dedicated folder for the driver components is considered good practice.

3. Utilize the appropriate commands within your MS-DOS environment to navigate to the directory containing the extracted or copied driver files. This will be the starting point for the installation process.

4. Identify and execute the main installation program within the driver directory. This is often named `INSTALL.EXE` or similar.

5. Carefully review and adhere to the on-screen prompts displayed during the installation process. These might involve:

    1. Pressing `Enter` to continue or confirm specific actions.
    2. Choosing the desired destination directory for the drivers. The suggested path (`C:\APPS\AWE64` in this instance) can be a suitable option if you lack specific preferences.
    3. Choosing between the provided Creative Configuration Manager (CTCM) or the alternative Intel PnP ISA Configuration Manager (ICM). While the guide recommends CTCM based on ease of use and availability, you may have specific reasons to choose ICM if compatible with your system.
    4. Reviewing the suggested installation settings and confirming their accuracy before proceeding.
    5. After completing the installation, a system reboot is usually necessary for the changes to take effect.

6. Following the reboot, navigate back to the directory containing the installed sound card drivers (e.g., `C:\APPS\AWE64` in this example).

7. Execute a diagnostic program like `DIAGNOSE.EXE` (if provided) to verify the sound card's proper functionality. This program will typically play test sounds, allowing you to confirm successful audio output.

8. If necessary, utilize additional utilities like `MIXERSET.EXE` to adjust sound levels and enable/disable features like 3D Stereo Enhancement based on your preferences.

Installing USB Drivers for MS-DOS

DOSUSB is an USB driver package for DOS. It consists of `DOSUSB.COM` - a TSR implementing a low level USB host controller driver (HCD/USBD), supporting EHCI, OHCI and UHCI controllers, and additional higher level drivers and code examples for storage media, printers and other devices.
There is also a special version available now which supports USB 3.0 with xHCI controllers. USB 3.0 ports support all USB speeds and therefore all kinds of devices. The current DOSUSB 3.0 version has been tested and works with USB 3.0 and 2.0 hard disks and flash disks. Other devices are still being tested and adapted. External hubs are not supported yet.
`DOSUSB.COM` provides a software layer so application programs and USB device drivers can be used supporting specific USB devices. With help of `DOSUSB.COM` it is possible for DOS application programs to communicate with all sorts of USB devices and to implement higher level USB device drivers for DOS.
DOSUSB can also be used with WIN 3.11. The `DOSUSB.COM` driver is supplied together with a DOS mass storage device driver for flash disks and memory card readers, a DOS printer device driver for printers connected via USB and a DOS device driver for USB serial port adapters.

Installation

1. Extract the zip file you have downloaded into a directory on your hard disk e.g. `c:\dosusb` . This directory will then contain three subdirectories and the following files:

DOSUSB.COM	The driver
USBVIEW.EXE	displays the descriptors of a USB device
LISTDEVS.EXE	Displays all devices and their addresses
LPT1USB.SYS	Device driver for printers replacing the LPT1: device

```
USBDISK.SYS            Device driver for mass storage
devices
SERDRV.SYS             Device driver for serial port
adapters
```

2. To start DOSUSB enter `DOSUSB.COM` a t the DOS prompt. DOSUSB will then enumerate all the connected devices and install itself as a resident program. It will display the controllers and devices found and show the address, speed plus Information about the devices.

DOSUSB itself requires about 30k of computer memory. However, it also requests additional memory for each controller installed in the computer. Running the EMM386 driver will speed up `DOSUSB.COM` significantly on some PCs.

DOSUSB offers a suite of drivers to bridge the gap between your modern computer and classic DOS applications. Here's a breakdown of its key functionalities:

Print directly from DOS applications using either `LPT1USB.SYS` or `PRNUSB.SYS`. These drivers work with various HP printers and parallel-to-USB adapters. Configure settings with the `SETALT` utility. `USBDISK.SYS` enables access to flash drives and USB hard disks. Load it with `DEVICE=` in your config.sys or use `DEVLOAD`. It assigns a drive letter and allows file management through standard DOS commands.

Notes:
MS-DOS 6.22 doesn't recognize FAT32 formatting, you'll need to use either DOS 7.0 or FreeDOS if your USB drive is formatted that way. Additionally, loading USBDISK.SYS in your CONFIG.SYS file might prevent the drive from being assigned a letter during boot. To avoid this, consider using DEVLOAD later on. Rebooting your system after swapping USB flash drives is also recommended to ensure data integrity. It's worth noting that the driver might not function with unformatted devices or require a partition table to be present on the drive.
Finally, there's SERDRV.SYS. This driver creates a "SERDRV" device that allows you to read and write to USB serial adapters using standard DOS commands. However, it's important to know that this driver works specifically with Prolific chipsets and might not be compatible with programs relying on serial interrupts.

Memory Optimization for Enhanced System Performance

Having successfully installed the necessary software, we now turn our attention to refining our system configuration and maximizing available conventional memory. This process ensures optimal performance for running various DOS applications and games.
As mentioned earlier, the `MEM /C /P` command provides a valuable tool for visualizing current memory consumption and remaining availability. In my case, despite

tweaking the configuration files and installing the listed software, only 497 KB of conventional memory remains free.

While this may seem adequate for certain applications, it falls short of the recommended threshold of >530 KB free memory. This higher threshold ensures compatibility with a wider range of DOS applications and games. It's important to note that this is not an absolute limit, and some programs may require even more free memory

Therefore, to accommodate a wider range of software and future installations, it's essential to further optimize our memory usage by employing various techniques. These techniques may involve: Disabling or removing unnecessary resident programs, adjusting configuration settings in certain applications to minimize their memory footprint, or utilizing memory managers that provide more efficient memory allocation strategies.

For reference, here's a sample `CONFIG.SYS` file at this point:

```
REM configure boot options
SWITCHES=/F
REM enable memory management
DEVICE=C:\DOS\HIMEM.SYS /TESTMEM:OFF
DEVICEHIGH=C:\DOS\EMM386.EXE RAM 24576
HIGHSCAN NOTR I=B000-B7FF
DOS=HIGH,UMB
REM load device drivers
DEVICEHIGH=C:\DOS\CDROMDRV.SYS /D:MSCD001
DEVICEHIGH=C:\DOS\NET\IFSHLP.SYS
DEVICEHIGH=C:\DOS\NET\PROTMAN.DOS
/I:C:\DOS\NET
DEVICEHIGH=C:\DOS\NET\NEMM.DOS
DEVICEHIGH=C:\DOS\NET\TCPDRV.DOS
DEVICEHIGH=C:\DOS\NET\ELNK3.DOS
DEVICEHIGH=C:\DOS\NET\DIS_PKT.DOS
DEVICEHIGH=C:\DOS\ANSI.SYS
DEVICEHIGH=C:\DOS\POWER ADV:MIN
DEVICE=C:\APPS\CTCM\CTCM.EXE
REM DEVICEHIGH=C:\DOS\SETVER.EXE
REM configure environment
SHELL=C:\DOS\COMMAND.COM C:\DOS /P
FILES=30
BUFFERS=5,0
FCBS=1
STACKS=0,0
```

```
LASTDRIVE=H
BREAK=on
```

SWITCHES=/F instructs the system to perform a fast boot, skipping non-essential checks during startup.
DEVICE=C:\DOS\HIMEM.SYS /TESTMEM:OFF enables the memory manager, responsible for allocating memory above the 1MB barrier and optimizing its utilization. /TESTMEM:OFF skips memory testing for faster boot times.
DEVICEHIGH=C:\DOS\EMM386.EXE RAM 24576 HIGHSCAN NOTR I=B000-B7FF , activates the EMM386.EXE memory manager, allowing the system to utilize extended memory (above 1MB) for various purposes like loading device drivers. The specified parameters configure settings like memory allocation size (RAM 24576), memory scanning mode (HIGHSCAN), and reserved memory regions (I=B000-B7FF).
DOS=HIGH,UMB instructs the system to load DOS itself into high memory for improved performance, leveraging the capabilities of the previously loaded memory managers.

Device Driver Loading:

A series of DEVICEHIGH commands load various device drivers, each serving a specific purpose:
CDROMDRV.SYS enables support for CD-ROM drives.
IFSHLP.SYS and PROTMAN.DOS are crucial for network functionality.
NEMM.DOS , TCPDRV.DOS , ELNK3.DOS , and DIS_PKT.DOS provide additional support for network communication protocols.
ANSI.SYS activates ANSI.SYS , allowing extended text and character display capabilities.
POWER ADV:MIN configures power management settings.
CTCM.EXE likely activates a specific application or device driver not directly related to core MS-DOS functionality.
While commented out (REM DEVICEHIGH=C:\DOS\SETVER.EXE), the line suggests potential use of the SETVER.EXE program, possibly for managing environment variables in specific scenarios.

Environment Configuration:

SHELL=C:\DOS\COMMAND.COM C:\DOS /P defines the default command shell used for user interaction.
FILES=30 specifies the maximum number of open files allowed at any given time.
BUFFERS=5,0 defines the number and size of disk buffers used to improve file access speed.
FCBS=1 sets the number of file control blocks, which manage open files.
STACKS=0,0 configures memory stacks used by programs.
LASTDRIVE=H specifies the highest available logical drive letter (H in this case).
BREAK=ON enables the ability to interrupt running programs using the CTRL+BREAK keyboard combination.
For reference, here's a sample AUTOEXEC.BAT file at this point:

```
@ECHO OFF
REM setup display and drivers
C:\DOS\MODE.COM CON COLS=80 LINES=50
LOADHIGH C:\DOS\MSCDEX.EXE /D:MSCD001
LOADHIGH C:\DOS\SMARTDRV.EXE
LOADHIGH C:\APPS\DOSKEY.COM -I
C:\DOS\CTMOUSE.EXE /3
REM setup network
REM LOADHIGH C:\DOS\3C5X9PD.COM 0X60
REM C:\DOS\NET\NET.EXE INITIALIZE
C:\DOS\NET\NETBIND.COM
C:\DOS\NET\UMB.COM
LOADHIGH C:\DOS\NET\TCPTSR.EXE
LOADHIGH C:\DOS\NET\TINYRFC.EXE
C:\DOS\NET\NMTSR.EXE
LOADHIGH C:\DOS\NET\EMSBFR.EXE
LOADHIGH C:\DOS\NET\DNR.EXE
C:\DOS\NET\NET START
REM setup sound card
SET SOUND=C:\APPS\AWE64
SET BLASTER=A220 I5 D1 H5 P330 E620 T6
SET MIDI=SYNTH:1 MAP:E MODE:0
SET CTCM=C:\APPS\AWE64\CTCM
C:\APPS\AWE64\DIAGNOSE.EXE /S
C:\APPS\AWE64\AWEUTIL.COM /S
C:\APPS\AWE64\MIXERSET.EXE /P /Q
C:\APPS\CTCM\CTCM.EXE /S
REM setup environment
PATH C:\APPS;C:\DOS;C:\DOS\NET
PROMPT $E[1;34M$P$G $E[0;47;0M
SET DIRCMD=/O:GNE
SET TEMP=C:\TEMP
SET WATTCP.CFG=C:\DOS\NET
ECHO.
```

Display and Drivers

@ECHO OFF: This line acts as a silent conductor, ensuring commands are executed without cluttering the screen with their echoes.

REM setup display and drivers: This comment serves as a helpful annotation, clarifying the purpose of the following lines.

C:\DOS\MODE.COM CON COLS=80 LINES=50: This command fine-tunes the display, adjusting the viewable area to 80 columns and 50 lines, providing a suitable canvas for your interactions.

LOADHIGH C:\DOS\MSCDEX.EXE /D:MSCD001 : This line, utilizing the
LOADHIGH command, loads the MSCDEX.EXE driver into high memory, optimizing
performance for CD-ROM access. The /D:MSCD001 argument specifies the device
driver letter for the CD-ROM drive.
LOADHIGH C:\DOS\SMARTDRV.EXE : Similar to the previous line, this command
loads the SMARTDRV driver into high memory, enhancing disk access speed and overall
system performance.
LOADHIGH C:\APPS\DOSKEY.COM -I : This line utilizes the LOADHIGH
command again, this time loading the DOSKEY program into high memory. The -I
argument instructs DOSKEY to complete command lines based on previously entered
commands, streamlining your workflow.
C:\DOS\CTMOUSE.EXE /3 : This command activates the CTMOUSE driver,
enabling you to interact with the graphical user interface using a mouse. The /3
argument specifies a specific mouse type.

Networking

REM LOADHIGH C:\DOS\3C5X9PD.COM 0x60 : This commented-out line, had it
been active, would have loaded a network card driver specific to the 3Com 5x9 series. The
0x60 argument defines the base memory address for the driver.
REM C:\DOS\NET\NET.EXE INITIALIZE : This commented-out line would have
initialized the network subsystem, preparing it for communication.
C:\DOS\NET\NETBIND.COM : This line binds the network card driver to a specific
network adapter, establishing the connection.
C:\DOS\NET\UMB.COM : This line activates the Upper Memory Block (UMB) driver,
providing additional memory for loading device drivers and applications.
LOADHIGH C:\DOS\NET\TCPTSR.EXE : This line loads the TCP/IP transport
protocol driver into high memory, enabling communication over TCP/IP networks .
LOADHIGH C:\DOS\NET\TINYRFC.EXE : This line loads a minimal TCP/IP stack
into high memory, offering basic network functionality.
C:\DOS\NET\NMTSR.EXE : This line loads the NetBEUI transport protocol driver into
high memory, enabling communication over NetBEUI networks.
LOADHIGH C:\DOS\NET\EMSBFR.EXE : This line loads a buffer manager into high
memory, improving network performance by optimizing memory usage.
LOADHIGH C:\DOS\NET\DNR.EXE : This line loads a driver for NetDDE, a
technology used for data exchange between applications on a network.
C:\DOS\NET\NET START : This line starts the network services, allowing you to
connect to other computers and access network resources.

Setting Up the Sound Card

SET SOUND=C:\APPS\AWE64 : This line defines the location of the AWE64 sound
card driver files.

`SET BLASTER=A220 I5 D1 H5 P330 E620 T6` : This line configures the sound card settings, specifying parameters like the I/O address, interrupt, DMA channel, and other hardware-specific details.

`SET MIDI=SYNTH:1 MAP:E MODE:0` : This line defines the MIDI configuration, specifying the synthesizer port, mapping mode, and mode number, ensuring compatibility with MIDI devices.

`SET CTCM=C:\APPS\AWE64\CTCM` : This line defines the location of the Creative Technology Configuration Manager (CTCM) program, responsible for managing the sound card's settings.

`C:\APPS\AWE64\DIAGNOSE.EXE /S` : This line executes the AWE64 diagnostic tool, verifying the sound card's functionality.

`C:\APPS\AWE64\AWEUTIL.COM /S` : This line executes the AWEUTIL which activates OPL3 output routing

In the realm of DOS, optimal startup sequence is important, as loading drivers and programs in random order can significantly inflate memory usage. Unfortunately, there exists no universally ideal sequence that guarantees the best outcome for every system. While the internet abounds with suggestions for tweaking DOS memory settings, the following three-pronged strategy has consistently yielded the most favorable results in my experience:

Employ a memory manager like `EMM386.EXE` to strategically load as many drivers and supplementary programs as possible into upper memory. This precious region offers greater benefits compared to conventional memory, alleviating memory constraints and enhancing ove rall system performance.

While `HIMEM.SYS` provides a solid foundation for memory management in DOS, some users might find themselves pushing the limits of available conventional memory. In such scenarios, exploring alternative memory managers can yield significant benefits. Two prominent options stand out: Jemm/HimemX and UMBPCI.

These third-party solutions boast a reputation for offering a wider range of advanced features while maintaining a more compact memory footprint compared to `HIMEM.SYS`. This translates to potentially greater efficiency in memory allocation, allowing you to squeeze more out of your system's available resources.

If you encounter situations where squeezing every last kilobyte of conventional memory is crucial to run specific programs or achieve a desired configuration, experimenting with Jemm/HimemX or UMBPCI is a worthwhile endeavor. Their advanced capabilities and potential for efficient memory utilization might be the key to unlocking the full potential of your DOS setup.

Prioritizing Large Drivers: In DOS, efficient memory management, particularly in upper memory, plays a crucial role in maximizing system performance. When loading device drivers, a strategic approach that prioritizes larger drivers can significantly improve upper memory utilization. This strategy leverages the way DOS allocates memory during program execution

Conventional Memory is the first 640KB of memory directly accessible by all programs. It's the most crucial but also the most limited memory area.

Upper Memory Blocks or UMBs is a memory region that resides above conventional memory and can be utilized by certain drivers and memory managers like HIMEM.SYS. However, UMBs are fragmented due to pre-allocated areas for system functions like video memory.
The High Memory Area or HMA exists above 1MB and can be accessed by some memory managers for specific purposes, but its usage can be less reliable compared to UMBs.
When loading device drivers, DOS allocates memory in "blocks" – contiguous segments within the UMB region. The size of these blocks can vary depending on existing allocations and fragmentation. Here's why prioritizing large drivers is beneficial
Larger drivers require bigger memory blocks. By loading them first, DOS fills larger gaps in the UMB area. This leaves smaller, more fragmented spaces remaining. Smaller drivers can then effectively utilize these smaller leftover gaps. This approach minimizes wasted memory within UMBs and maximizes overall memory utilization.
By maximizing UMB utilization, more memory remains available for applications and reduces conflicts between drivers competing for limited space. Efficient memory management can enhance system stability by minimizing memory allocation errors and conflicts. With more available memory for programs, overall system performance can improve.

Imagine UMBs as a series of empty boxes of varying sizes. Placing large boxes (drivers) first ensures they fit neatly in the bigger spaces. This leaves smaller boxes (drivers) to fill the remaining gaps more efficiently, minimizing wasted space.

Note: While prioritizing large drivers is a generally sound strategy, it's not a foolproof solution. With complex memory fragmentation, even large drivers might not perfectly fit remaining gaps, leading to some wasted space. Additionally, driver dependencies may require loading specific drivers in a certain order regardless of size.

Whe never feasible, opt for smaller drivers – akin to the approach taken with the CD-ROM and mouse drivers discussed earlier. Streamlining driver size translates to a reduced footprint in memory, leaving more resources available for applications and improving overall system efficiency.
Each loaded driver occupies a contiguous block of memory in the conventional memory space. By minimizing driver size, we can decrease the amount of memory they consume. This directly translates to a larger pool of memory available for applications and the operating system itself.
As you load and unload programs in DOS, memory becomes fragmented – scattered blocks of free and used memory interspersed throughout the address space. When loading new drivers, the operating system needs to locate a contiguous block large enough to accommodate the driver. Smaller drivers are easier to fit into these fragmented gaps, minimizing the likelihood of memory becoming unusable due to excessive fragmentation.

When loading the operating system and initializing devices, DOS needs to locate and execute the necessary drivers. Smaller drivers generally require less time to load and process, leading to quicker system startup times. Additionally, context switching between applications might benefit as smaller drivers take less time to swap in and out of memory during task changes.

While smaller drivers are generally preferable, it's important to strike a balance. Overly simplified drivers might lack essential functionality required for proper device operation. Finding drivers that offer the necessary features while maintaining a compact size is ideal. Some driver developers employ techniques to further optimize memory usage. This can involve code compression or utilizing memory overlays, where only a portion of the driver is loaded into memory at a time, with the remaining code being swapped in as needed.

While DOS offers a built-in utility called MEMMAKER designed to automate memory optimization, its attempts at achieving optimal settings yielded slightly inferior results compared to the manually configured files described above. Nevertheless, I encourage experimentation with MEMMAKER. It's possible that on your specific hardware configuration, MEMMAKER might produce superior outcomes. Additionally, even if it doesn't provide the absolute best results, it offers a convenient undo function to easily revert any changes made.

Exploring Optional Software

With the base installation of MS-DOS 6.22 up and running, complete with network connectivity and essential utilities, we have established a robust and optimized foundation. This stable environment, compatible in large part with Windows for Workgroups 3.11 (aside from potential network driver adjustments), serves as your springboard for further customization. You're now empowered to explore and install a vast array of additional applications, games, utilities, and drivers, tailoring the system to your specific needs and preferences. In this section, we'll delve into some particularly useful and captivating software options that may enrich your experience.

Enhance Your DOS Experience with 4DOS

4DOS is a powerful replacement shell for the standard DOS command interpreter, command.com. Offering a multitude of significant enhancements, it empowers you to navigate your DOS environment with greater efficiency and control. Additionally, 4DOS boasts remarkable cust omization capabilities, allowing you to tailor the experience to your specific needs.

While initially commercially available, 4DOS has entered the realm of open source software, ensuring its continued ava ilability and fostering ongoing development. The open-source iteration, often referred to as Free 4DOS, remains actively maintained, currently residing at version 8.00. This is the recommended version, readily available from the official website.

Installation Made Simple

1. Begin by extracting the downloaded archive (ensure it is unzipped).
2. Subsequently, copy the entire directory to the designated location, typically `C:\APPS\4DOS`.
3. Once the files are in place, navigate to the directory using the cd command and execute the program by typing `4DOS.COM`.
4. Follow the on-screen prompts to complete the installation.

By default, the installation offers the option to automatically update your existing `AUTOEXEC.BAT` and `CONFIG.SYS` files. However, for greater control and customization, you can opt to manually edit these files.

5. Open the `AUTOEXEC.BAT` file in a text editor
6. append the following lines, replacing existing entries if necessary:

```
REM LOADHIGH C:\APPS\DOSKEY.COM -I
C:\APPS\4DOS\KSTACK.COM
```

`REM LOADHIGH C:\APPS\DOSKEY.COM -I` : This line instructs the system to load the `DOSKEY.COM` program in high memory, a technique for maximizing available memory in DOS. The `-I` parameter enables line editing functionality, allowing you to recall and modify previous comman ds.
`C:\APPS\4DOS\KSTACK.COM` : This line loads the kstack.com program, a utility offered by 4DOS that enhances keyboard functionality.

7. Open the `CONFIG.SYS` file in a text editor
8. Replace the existing SHELL command with the following:

```
SHELL=C:\APPS\4DOS\4DOS.COM C:\APPS\4DOS /P
```

`SHELL=C:\APPS\4DOS\4DOS.COM C:\APPS\4DOS /P` : specifies that 4DOS will become the default shell used by the system. The `/P` parameter ensures that the initial drive and directory are displayed upon startup, providing a familiar starting point.

Streamlining Your 4DOS Setup

4DOS provides a robust command-line experience out of the box, incorporating tab completion and command history, eliminating the need for the external utility "Enhanced DOSKEY.com." While 4DOS currently lacks the functionality to complete commands based on your path as you type (a feature commonly referred to as path completion), it offers various other enhancements.

Similarly, " KSTACK.COM " is only necessary if you intend to utilize the 4DOS command "KEYSTACK." For those unfamiliar with this command, you can access its help by running HELP KEYSTACK . If this functionality isn't required, you can safely comment out the "kstack.com" line in your configuration file to conserve memory.

To personalize your 4DOS experience, you can leverage the built-in "option.exe" utility. This tool offers extensive customization options, allowing you to tailor various aspects of the program's behavior. Here are some recommended non-default settings that I have found particularly beneficial:

Configuration > Startup:

Set " Resident in UMB" to Yes (This enables 4DOS to load into Upper Memory Blocks, potentially improving performance and freeing up conventional memory.)
Swapping: Configure this setting based on your system's available memory and preferences. Options include XMS (Extended Memory Swap), EMS (Expanded Memory Swap), or None.

Configuration > Display:

Tabs: Set the desired number of spaces for tab characters. (Here, the example sets it to 4 spaces.)

Configuration > Command Line:

Default Mode: Insert (This mode allows you to insert text within existing commands, which can be helpful for editing.)
Cursor: Overstrike: Set the percentage of character width used for the overstrike cursor in overtype mode. (Here, the example sets it to 100%.)
Cursor: Insert: Set the percentage of character width used for the block cursor in insert mode. (Here, the example sets it to 10%.)
Move to End: Yes (This enables the ability to quickly move the cursor to the end of the current line.)
Exit > Save: After making your adjustments, remember to save the configuration changes within " OPTION.EXE ."

Extending Command Functionality with Aliases in 4DOS

One valuable feature offered by 4DOS is the ability to create aliases , similar to the concept found in Linux. These aliases act as convenient shortcuts, allowing you to execute existing commands with a shorter or more user-friendly name.

For those unfamiliar with aliases, their functionality can be best understood through a practical example. Enter the command `ALIAS LS=DIR /WBH` followed by `LS` . If successful, you should observe a directory listing formatted identically to the default `LS` command in Linux. This might seem like a simple application, but the power of aliases lies in their ability to streamline numerous tasks.

Consider the following sample configuration file, `ALIASES.CFG` , as an illustration:

```
DIR=*DIR %DIRCMD
LS=DIR /WBH
RM=DEL
MV=MOVE
CP=COPY
CAT=TYPE
DATE=ECHO %_DATE %_TIME
EJECT=EJECTMEDIA
VI=EDIT
P=XFSTOOL.EXE PKTDRV STOP ^ %1 %2 %3 %4 %5 %6
%7 %8 %9 ^ XFSTOOL.EXE PKTDRV RESTART
MOVED=MKDIR %2\%@NAME[%1] ^ XCOPY /E %1
%2\%@NAME[%1] ^ DELTREE %1
REALIAS=UNALIAS * ^ ALIAS /R
D:\ETC\ALIASES.CFG
```

In this configuration:

`DIR=*DIR %DIRCMD` : This alias ensures that whenever you type `DIR` , the system first attempts to execute a custom command defined by the environment variable `%DIRCMD` . If no such command exists, the default dir command is used.

`LS` , `RM` , `MV` , `CP` , `CAT` , `DATE` , `EJECT` , and `VI` : These aliases provide shortcuts for existing commands, making them easier and quicker to type.

`P` :   This intricate alias defines a custom command sequence using the `XFSTOOL.EXE` utility to stop a specific partition, followed by restarting it.

`MOVED` : This complex alias creates a directory structure, copies files from the source directory to the newly created structure, and then deletes the original source directory.

`REALIAS` : This alias serves a maintenance function, clearing all existing aliases before reloading them from the `D:\ETC\ALIASES.CFG` file.

Delving Deeper into 4DOS Enhancements:

While many of the aforementioned commands offer convenient shortcuts, a select few warrant further exploration:

`DIR` : This command ensures 4DOS adheres to the DIR command flags specified within the `DIRCMD` variable. As a result, consistent default behavior is maintained regardless of whether 4DOS is loaded or not, streamlining your directory listing preferences.

`DATE` : This streamlined command directly outputs the current date and time, eliminating the need for unnecessary prompts to set it, providing a more efficient approach to retrieving date/time information.

`EJECT` : This command leverages a built-in 4DOS functionality to eject the CD-ROM drive, offering a quick and convenient way to remove discs without relying on external methods.

`P` : As mentioned earlier in the NFS/XFS section, prepending the letter "p" to any command instructs 4DOS to perform a specific sequence. It temporarily unloads the XFS packet driver before executing the given command (e.g., `P SSH USERNAME SERVER` for SSH access) and then reloads the driver upon completion. This enables you to seamlessly utilize commands like SSH even while an NFS share is mounted, addressing potential driver conflicts.

`MOVED` : This command represents the most effective method I've discovered for effortlessly transferring directories between locations. While it may not be entirely foolproof, it remains a valuable tool. I remain open to suggestions for further improvements to this command.

`REALIAS` : This command efficiently reloads your alias file, ensuring any newly added or modified aliases become active within 4DOS.

While using an alias file is entirely optional, I find it beneficial to have all aliases conveniently grouped together for easy reference and management. To activate this functionality, simply add the command `ALIAS /R C:\APPS\ALIASES.CFG` (or your preferred file path) to your `AUTOEXEC.BAT` file, ensuring the aliases are loaded automatically upon system startup.

Enhancing Directory Readability with Colorized Listings (Optional)

While not strictly essential, an interesting customization option exists for those who appreciate a touch of visual flair: enabling colored directory listings. This functionality, familiar to users of modern Linux distributions (as exemplified below), allows for the quick and effortless distinction of different file types at a single glance.

```
COLORDIR=DIRS:BRI BLUE;HIDDEN:BRI BLA;EXE COM DOS:BRI
GRE;BAT BTM CMD:GRE;ZIP TGZ:BRI RED;JPG GIF BMP PNG ICO:BRI
```

```
MAG;MOV MPG:MAG;MID MP3 WAV:BRI CYA;TXT DOC ME NOW 1ST DIZ
CFG INF INI:BRI YELLOW;*~* BAK:YEL
```

In this example, directories appear in blue, text files in white, and images and audio files are distinguished by unique colorations. This configuration mirrors the default scheme of Linux's `DIRCOLORS` utility, albeit with slight modifications and adjustments for brevity.

The provided configuration string, while concise, follows a clear structure:
List of extensions: This specifies the file extensions associated with a particular file type. For instance, `TXT DOC ME NOW 1ST DIZ CFG INF INI` represents various text file extensions.
Colon delimiter (":"): This separates the extensions from the color code.
Color code: This defines the color to be applied to the listed file types. The provided configuration utilizes various color codes like `BRI BLUE` for bright blue and `GRE` for green.
Semicolon delimiter (";"): This separates each colorized file type entry from the next.

By implementing this configuration, you can enhance the visual appeal and informativeness of your directory listings, similar to the experience offered by modern operating systems. Remember that this customization step is entirely optional and primarily serves aesthetic purposes.

Advanced Customization with Directory Listings and 4DOS.INI

Beyond assigning a single color to the entire directory listing, 4DOS allows for further customization through extension lists and color combinations.

Extension Lists: The initial element in the provided line, dirs, functions as an extension list. This specifies that the following color settings apply specifically to directories within the listing. Other examples of extension lists include `HIDDEN` which applies the color settings to hidden files and `RDONLY` which applies the color settings to read-only files.

Color Flexibility: As demonstrated, you can utilize both standard colors (e.g., `YEL`) and bright colors (e.g., `BRI YEL`) for customization. Bright colors generally offer improved readability against darker backgrounds.

Background Color: The command extends beyond text color by also allowing adjustments to the character background color. For instance, `BRI BLU ON YEL` displays blue text on a yellow background.

Implementation and Customization:

1. Run the provided command with the set command, followed by dir to test the applied colors.
2. Once satisfied with the customization, you have two options for persistence:

    1. Prepend the command with `SET` and add it to your `AUTOEXEC.BAT` file. However, this approach can potentially clutter your environment variables.
    2. Simply copy the command as-is to the `C:\4DOS\4DOS.INI` file. This is the recommended approach. Further Exploration:

Note: For exploring more advanced functionalities offered by 4DOS, consult the comprehensive documentation accessible through the `HELP` command. To access the original MS-DOS help pages, utilize the command `HELP.COM`

Exploring the Web with Arachne: A Graphical Browser for Your DOS System

While DOS is primarily known for its text-based interface, a surprising gem exists for those seeking a graphical web browsing experience: Arachne. While modern web standards may not be fully supported due to inherent limitations, navigating the basic web remains quite feasible with this browser.

Obtaining Arachne is straightforward; simply visit its official homepage. Installing Arachne requires some attention to detail, although the process itself isn't overly complex. The primary challenge lies in the demanding memory requirement: a minimum of 500 KB of free conventional RAM. If you've followed the previous system optimization recommendations, this might not be an issue. However, if you fall short, kindly refer back to the optimization section for guidance on freeing up the necessary memory. Additionally, a mouse is essential for navigating Arachne, so ensure you have a functional mouse driver installed as described earlier.

Installing Arachne

1. Once you confirm at least 500 KB of free conventional memory using the `MEM /C /P` command, initiate the setup process by running `A195GPL.EXE`. Follow the on-screen prompts carefully. For consistency with the installation structure outlined in this guide, it's recommended to choose a custom installation

path of `C:\APPS\ARACHNE` when prompted. Simply press N and modify the directory before proceeding.

2. Upon successful unpacking of the files, the graphical installer will launch. Be aware that if you have only a marginal amount of free memory exceeding the 500 KB threshold, the installer might encounter a "low memory" error. This occurs because the memory used by the unpacking process remains temporarily in use, pushing you below the minimum requirement. In such a scenario, simply execute `C:\APPS\ARACHNE\ARACHNE.BAT` to restart the graphical setup wizard.

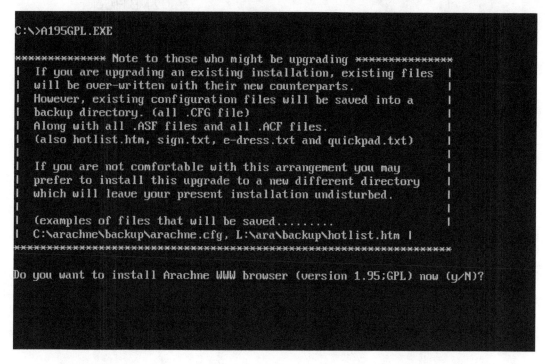

```
C:\>A195GPL.EXE

************** Note to those who might be upgrading ***************
I  If you are upgrading an existing installation, existing files  I
I  will be over-written with their new counterparts.              I
I  However, existing configuration files will be saved into a     I
I  backup directory. (all .CFG file)                              I
I  Along with all .ASF files and all .ACF files.                  I
I  (also hotlist.htm, sign.txt, e-dress.txt and quickpad.txt)     I
I                                                                 I
I  If you are not comfortable with this arrangement you may       I
I  prefer to install this upgrade to a new different directory    I
I  which will leave your present installation undisturbed.        I
I                                                                 I
I  (examples of files that will be saved........                  I
I  C:\arachne\backup\arachne.cfg, L:\ara\backup\hotlist.htm I
*******************************************************************

Do you want to install Arachne WWW browser (version 1.95;GPL) now (y/N)?
```

3. **Video Options:** Tailor your visual experience by adjusting the video settings. Aim for a resolution of at least 1024x768, or even higher if your monitor's size allows and your video card boasts sufficient memory. However, be aware that the capabilities of your video card will ultimately determine the maximum achievable resolution. If you encounter any difficulties during the setup process and need to restart, simply execute the `C:\APPS\ARACHNE\SETUP.BAT` file again.

Arachne detected video adapter:

VESA

■ CGA 640x200 16 KB 2 shades

■ EGA 640x350 128 KB 16 colors

□ VESA compatible card or driver

■ VGA 640x480 256 KB 16 colors

■ VGA 640x480 256 KB grayscale

■ TRIDENT (or PROVGA_VC510S)

■ TSG3 (Tseng ET3000, MDB10)

■ OAK

■ REALTEK (RTVGA)

■ TSG4 (Tseng ET4000)

■ M1 (OCTEK, graphic chip MX86010)

■ TAMARA (Tamarack TDVGA-3588,
   Cirrus, Paradise, AST-PLUS)

■ 640x480	1 MB HiColor
■ 800x600	1 MB HiColor
■ 1024x768	2 MB HiColor
■ 640x400	256 KB 256 colors
□ 640x480	512 KB 256 colors
■ 800x600	512 KB 256 colors
■ 1024x768	1 MB 256 colors
■ 800x600	256 KB 16 colors
■ 800x600	256 KB grayscale

Try selected graphics mode

1) Pick the default setup by clicking on "Try selected graphics mode" (Recommended for beginners)
... alternately....
2a) Pick a card type by tabbing to appropriate check box and pressing enter..or..'leftclick' on appropriate check box.
2b) Pick a size/color resolution in the same manner (tab/enter or leftclick).
2c) Tab/Enter or leftclick on "Try selected graphics mode".

4. **Computer Speed:** Arachne offers a recommended computer speed profile, determined after a quick benchmark of your system. This option is likely the most suitable for achieving optimal performance. Choose your preferred profile and proceed by clicking "Next."

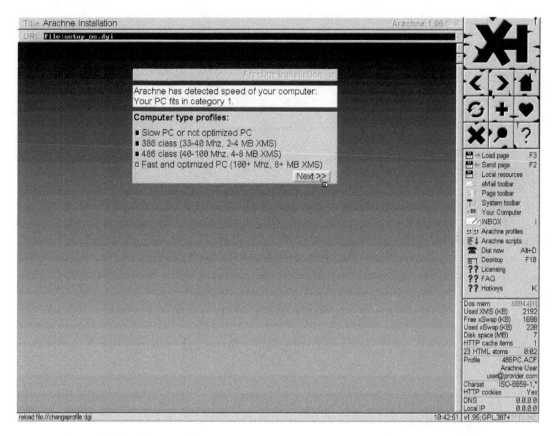

5. **System Configuration:** Personalize your experience further by configuring the system settings. Here, you have complete control over various options, such as automatic or manual file updates after installation and creation of shortcut batch files. Select the options that align with your preferences and click "Next." Ensure the maximum video resolution matches the one you selected earlier and click "Next" once more.

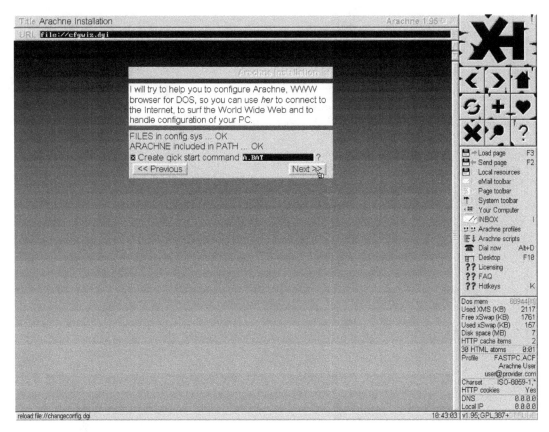

6. **Network Configuration:** Assuming you have a functional WATTCP configuration, select the "Manual Setup" option when prompted for network configuration. Next, choose "Resident packet driver" followed by "Use only WATTCP configuration." Enter the path to your WATTCP configuration file, which is typically located at C:\APPS\WATTCP.CFG , and click "Save."

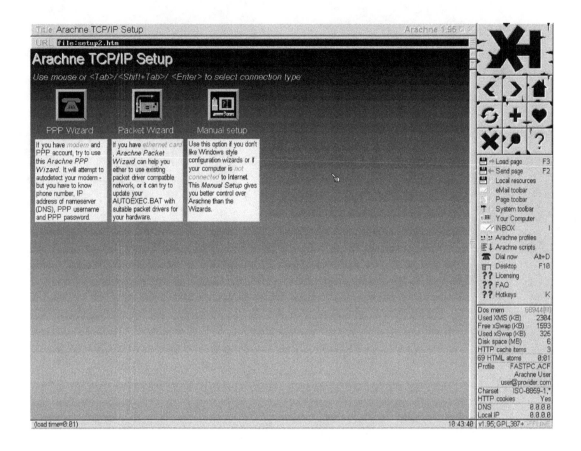

7. **Arachne Options:** While the "Arachne Options" page allows for customization at any time, you can finalize the setup process by selecting "Use new settings." This will return you to the DOS prompt, presenting you with an opportunity to adjust your system configuration files. If you opted not to have Arachne update the `CONFIG.SYS` file during setup, consider modifying the `FILES` variable to 40.

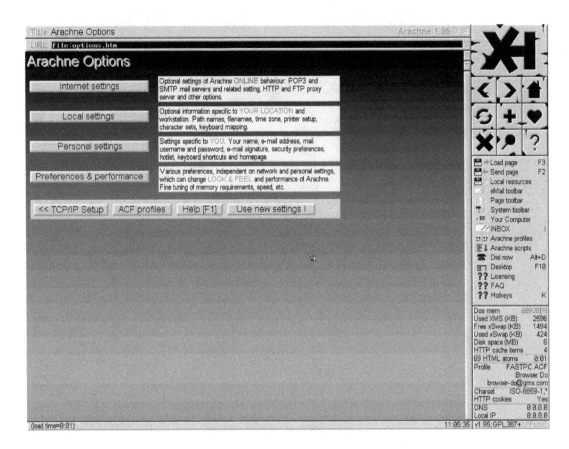

Refining Your Arachne Experience

Having conquered the initial installation, let's explore some ways to optimize and personalize your Arachne setup for a smoother journey on the web.

Streamlining Access: Remember that handy shortcut we created during installation? Now's the time to relocate it for maximum convenience. An ideal spot would be your C:\APPS directory. This placement has a hidden benefit: it automatically adds the directory to your system's PATH . With this trick, you can simply type "ARACHNE" at the command prompt, and Arachne will spring to life, no need to navigate through folders!

To achieve this feat, head over to the directory containing the ARACHNE.BAT file (usually within C:\APPS\ARACHNE). There, type the following command, substituting " C:\APPS\ARACHNE\A.BAT " with the actual location of your ARACHNE.BAT file:

```
MOVE C:\APPS\ARACHNE\A.BAT
C:\APPS\ARACHNE.BAT
```

Ensuring File Association Magic: If you tinkered with your system's FILES settings during installation, a quick reboot is highly recommended. This reboot ensures those changes take full effect, allowing Arachne to seamlessly handle all your internet-related tasks.

Testing the Web Waters: With these adjustments in place, launch Arachne by typing "ARACHNE" at the command prompt. Now, the moment of truth! Let's test your internet connection. Navigate to a website like WWW.GOOGLE.COM. Don't be surprised by the lack of modern graphical bells and whistles, but the website's content should be displayed in its entirety, proving you're connected to the vast web.

Unleashing Customization Magic: Arachne isn't a one-size-fits-all browser. It offers a treasure trove of options to tailor your browsing experience. From adjusting the layout for better readability, to tweaking performance for a smoother ride, the possibilities are vast.

Ready to delve into these settings? Access the "Desktop" link nestled in the right-hand navigation bar (or press F10). From the available menu choices, select "Options." Here, you can unleash your inner tinkerer and customize Arachne to your heart's content, transforming it into a truly personalized and efficient web explorer.

Advanced arachne configuration

In MS-DOS, a RAMdisk (or RAM drive) is a clever way to utilize your computer's memory for storage. Imagine carving out a section of your RAM and turning it into a virtual hard drive. This offers a significant speed advantage because accessing data in RAM is much faster than on a physical hard disk with spinning platters. However, there's a catch: RAM is volatile memory. Anything stored on your RAMdisk disappears when you turn off your computer or reboot MS-DOS.

While not essential for everyday use, RAMdisks can be beneficial for specific tasks. For instance, storing frequently used program files on a RAMdisk can lead to noticeable performance gains, making your favorite game load in a flash compared to the usual wait times from a physical drive. Additionally, RAMdisks can help protect your hard drive. Frequent read/write operations can cause wear and tear. By using a RAMdisk for temporary files or data-intensive tasks, you can offload some of the workload from your hard drive, potentially extending its lifespan. Another benefit is disk caching. A RAMdisk can store frequently accessed data from your physical drive, making it readily available in RAM and boosting overall system performance.

Setting up a RAMdisk in MS-DOS involves using a device driver called RAMDRIVE.SYS. This driver, loaded in your CONFIG.SYS file, allows you to configure the size and memory location of your RAMdisk. However, there's a trade-off to consider. The RAM allocated to your RAMdisk becomes unavailable for running programs, so finding the right balance between RAMdisk size and system performance is crucial.

If your MS-DOS system boasts a generous 12MB or more of RAM, you can leverage a RAMdisk to significantly enhance Arachne's performance.by doing the following:

Creating the RAMdisk: While assigning drive letters seems straightforward (A: and B: for floppies, C: for the primary partition), it's worth a quick verification. Reboot your system after adding the RAMdisk configuration to your `CONFIG.SYS` file (details below). Observe the drive letter assigned – in our example, it's E:.

RAMdisk Size: The more RAM you allocate to the RAMdisk, the better. Web browser caches, for instance, can balloon in size during extended browsing sessions. Here, we'll create a 12MB RAMdisk (remember, the maximum size for RAMDRIVE.SYS is 32,767 KB).

Adding the RAMdisk Configuration: To create the RAMdisk, add the following string to your CONFIG.SYS file (somewhere in the middle):

```
DEVICE=C:\DOS\RAMDRIVE.SYS 12000 512 512 /E
```

Explanation of Parameters:
DEVICE=C:\DOS\RAMDRIVE.SYS: Specifies the location of the RAMDRIVE.SYS driver.
12000: Denotes the size of the RAMdisk in KB (12,000 KB in this case).
512: Defines the sector size (usually 512 bytes).
512: Sets the number of clusters per allocation unit.
/E: Assigns the drive letter "E" to the RAMdisk.

Arachne on RAMdisk (Preserving Downloads): Since the RAMdisk is cleared upon reboot, any files installed directly on it will be lost. To avoid this with essential Arachne files, we'll create a folder structure on your physical hard drive (C: drive in this case).
Create a folder named "ARACHNE" on drive C:. Within this folder, create another subfolder named "DOWNLOAD". The DOWNLOAD folder will house any files downloaded by Arachne, ensuring they persist across reboots.

Arachne Configuration for RAMdisk: Now, we need to configure Arachne to use the newly created folders on the hard drive. Edit the `ARACHNE.CFG` file and specify the following paths:

> DownloadPath: Set this to `C:\ARACHNE\DOWNLOAD` to direct downloaded files to the dedicated folder.
> Cookies.lst: Set this to `C:\ARACHNE\COOKIES.LST` to manage cookies on the hard drive.

ARACHNE.BAT Modification: The `ARACHNE.BAT` script is responsible for launching Arachne. We'll need to modify it to function correctly with the RAMdisk. Edit the `ARACHNE.BAT` file and replace its contents with the following:

```
@ECHO OFF
LH C:\SOFT\NET\PCIPKT.COM 0X60
COPY C:\DOS\COMMAND.COM E:
SET COMSPEC=E:\COMMAND.COM
E:
CD E:\ARACHNE
```

```
ARACHNE.BAT %1 %2 %3 %4
C:
SET COMSPEC=C:\DOS\COMMAND.COM
```

Explanation of Changes:

The script first loads the network packet driver (`PCIPKT.COM`) as usual.

It then copies a copy of `COMMAND.COM` (the MS-DOS shell) to the RAMdisk (drive E:).
The script temporarily sets the system's command processor (`COMSPEC`) to the copied
version on the RAMdisk.

It changes the current directory to the Arachne installation folder on the RAMdisk (
`E:\ARACHNE`).

The script then launches the actual Arachne program (`ARACHNE.BAT`) along with any
provided command-line arguments.

Finally, after Arachne exits, the script switches the `COMSPEC` back to the original version
on the hard drive and returns to the C: drive.

Backing Up the RAMdisk Contents (Optional):
For added convenience, you can
create a compressed archive of the entire `E:\ARACHNE` folder contents after
configuration. Here, we'll create an archive named " `A.ZIP` " on your `C:` drive using
PKZIP:

```
C:\PKZIP -PR C:\A.ZIP E:\ARACHNE\*.*
```

Automating RAMdisk Setup in AUTOEXEC.BAT:
Finally, edit your
AUTOEXEC.BAT file and add the following lines somewhere in the middle:

```
MKDIR E:\TEMP
SET TEMP=E:\TEMP
SET ARACHNETEMP=E:\TEMP
MKDIR E:\ARACHNE
PKUNZIP -D C:\A.ZIP E:\ARACHNE
```

Explanation:

```
MKDIR E:\TEMP: Creates a temporary folder on the RAMdisk
SET TEMP=E:\TEMP: Sets the environment variable for
temporary files
SET ARACHNETEMP=E:\TEMP: Sets another environment variable
for Arachne's temporary files
MKDIR E:\ARACHNE: Creates the Arachne folder on the RAMdisk
PKUNZIP -D C:\A.ZIP E:\ARACHNE: Extracts the Arachne archive
onto the RAMdisk
```

Exploring the System with Navrátil Software

Delving deeper into the inner workings of your computer can reveal valuable insights and empower you to troubleshoot potential issues. Amongst the various tools I encountered during my research, Navrátil Software System Information stands out as a truly exceptional utility.

This comprehensive program gathers and presents detailed information about the intricate components that make up your system. From intricate details about your processor and memory to a thorough analysis of storage devices and network adapters, Navrátil paints a clear picture of your computer's hardware configuration.

What truly sets it apart is its unwavering commitment to remaining completely free and unencumbered by limitations, a rarity in the realm of system information utilities. Furthermore, its active development ensures continued support and ongoing improvements, making it a reliable companion for your technological explorations.

As an added bonus, Navrátil Software provides a basic CPU benchmark, allowing you to gauge the processing power of your system. Whether you're simply curious about your computer's capabilities or troubleshooting potential performance issues, this versatile utility offers valuable insights.

if you've ever wondered about the inner workings of your system or sought to understand its performance, I highly recommend exploring the capabilities of Navrátil Software System Information. It stands as a testament to both comprehensive functionality and unwavering commitment to user accessibility.

MS-DOS Screenshot Utilities: Snarf and Screen Thief

For those undertaking visual documentation within the MS-DOS environment, the selection of suitable screenshot utilities is limited. This review explores two such options: Snarf and Screen Thief.

Snarf presents itself as a straightforward utility, lacking extensive configuration options. However, in my testing, it delivered dependable performance, capturing the screen contents effectively. This simplicity may appeal to users seeking a no-frills solution for basic screenshot capture.

Screen Thief, conversely, boasts a wider array of features, potentially catering to users with more diverse needs. However, a notable drawback emerged during my evaluation. While functional, the captured images displayed an unexpected horizontal stretch, presenting a distorted aspect ratio. This appears to be inherent behavior, as attempts to modify the output resolution proved unsuccessful. This unintended consequence renders Screen Thief unsuitable for my specific requirements, prioritizing faithful representation of the captured screen.

Ultimately, the choice between these utilities rests upon individual needs and preferences. While Snarf offers a streamlined approach, Screen Thief's feature set might hold appeal for users seeking additional functionalities. However, the aforementioned distortion issue in Screen Thief necessitates careful consideration before adoption, particularly when accurate image preservation is paramount.

Remote Access Options for DOS Systems

In our exploration of DOS networking, we stumbled upon a unique tool called RMENU. The author describes it as a "kind of" telnet server for DOS, allowing for remote control of a DOS machine via the ubiquitous telnet protocol. This application offers a menu-driven interface for easier navigation, alongside the familiar command line access.

While its practical use cases might be somewhat limited in today's world, RMENU certainly presents itself as a viable and well-crafted solution for those seeking remote access capabilities within a DOS environment.

However, it's essential to acknowledge the existence of alternative options like Remoter and Tiny. Unfortunately, Remoter requires a dedicated Windows client, rendering it unsuitable for our purposes. Similarly, Tiny necessitates the use of either the Novell or PCTCP TCP/IP stack, which are outside the scope of our current network configuration. This limitation excludes Tiny from further consideration.

RMENU emerges as the optimal choice given the constraints of our existing setup. It's worth noting that the RMENU author also offers a range of additional DOS applications, potentially holding further utility. These can be accessed through the same source mentioned previously.

ANSIPLUS: A Comprehensive Console Enhancement

ANSIPLUS expands upon the functionality of the previously discussed ANSI.SYS driver, offering a significantly enhanced experience for users working within the confines of the MS-DOS command line. Think of it as a comprehensive upgrade to your console environment.

Unlike its predecessor, ANSIPLUS integrates numerous features that would typically necessitate separate utilities, streamlining your workflow and providing a more robust and unified environment. These features include:

Scroll Back Buffer: No longer will lost lines of text disappear into the abyss. ANSIPLUS keeps a record of previous lines, allow ing you to review past commands and output with ease.

Extended Keyboard Input Buffer: Say goodbye to the frustration of accidentally typing over uncompleted commands. The expanded buffer provides you wi th more space to compose and edit your input before execution.

Mouse Support for Console Copy/Paste: This feature eliminates the need for complex keyboard combinations. With   ANSIPLUS , you can utilize your mouse to effortlessly copy and paste text within the console environment, enhancing efficiency and user-friendliness.

While installation and configuration might require a bit more effort compared to standard drivers, the comprehensive documentation provided in the ansiplus.doc manual will guide you through the process. Investing some time in the initial setup will unlock the significant benefits that   ANSIPLUS   offers to enhance your MS-DOS experience.

Utilizing SLOWDOWN for Retro Gaming

For enthusiasts of classic software, particularly games, a unique challenge arises – the ever-increasing processing power of modern computers. These older titles, often designed for environments with significantly slower CPUs, can become unplayable due to their inherent reliance on cycle timing for proper execution. To bridge this gap, specialized utilities exist, aptly named slowdown utilities, to artificially throttle the processing power of your machine.

Amongst these solutions stands SLOWDOWN , a freely available and feature-rich utility that effectively addresses this very issue. Its intuitive interface and comprehensive documentation make it a user-friendly choice for those seeking to revisit the golden age of gaming.

One particularly noteworthy feature within SLOWDOWN is the CPUCACHE utility. This tool allows you to disable your CPU's cache, a critical component in modern processors but often detrimental to the performance of older software. During my own exploration with Wing Commander, this approach proved to be the most effective in achieving consistent gameplay speed and a truly authentic experience.

Beyond SLOWDOWN , the author's website offers a treasure trove of additional utilities, including native DOS USB drivers. These tools further empower you to seamlessly integrate modern peripherals with your retro computing setup.

If you're venturing into the world of classic software, SLOWDOWN and its accompanying utilities are invaluable companions on your journey. They provide the crucial control needed to bridge the gap between modern hardware and the timeless enjoyment offered by these retro gems.

A Nostalgic Farewell and a Look Ahead

As we reach the end of our exploration of MS-DOS, a wave of nostalgia might wash over you. This operating system, though no longer at the forefront of computing, played a pivotal role in shaping the digital landscape. It empowered users, fostered creativity, and laid the foundation for the modern personal computer experience.

The skills you've acquired throughout this book have equipped you to navigate the inner workings of MS-DOS, optimize your system, and delve into its potential. Whether you're a seasoned user revisiting a familiar friend or a newcomer embarking on a journey of discovery, MS-DOS offers valuable lessons that transcend its era.

While MS-DOS may not be the dominant force it once was, the knowledge you've gained extends far beyond its command prompt. Understanding the core principles of operating systems, memory management, and configuration serves as a stepping stone to comprehending modern computing systems.

The concepts you've grasped can be applied to navigating more advanced operating systems, troubleshooting technical issues, and appreciating the evolution of technology. So, as you move forward, take with you the valuable knowledge and the sense of accomplishment gained from your exploration of MS-DOS. Remember, the skills you've honed here are not relics of the past, but building blocks for the future.

Looking Ahead: Building Upon Your Foundation

The world of technology is ever-evolving. While MS-DOS may not be the primary operating system of today, the knowledge you've acquired provides a solid foundation for further exploration. Consider these potential paths:

Your experience with batch files can be a springboard for learning more advanced scripting languages and programming fundamentals. If you crave the nostalgia of MS-DOS, explore emulators that allow you to run the operating system on modern computers. This can be a fun way to revisit classic games and software.

Remember, the journey of learning is a continuous process. The knowledge you've gained from MS-DOS is not an endpoint, but rather a stepping stone on your path to becoming a more informed and tech-savvy user.

A Final Note: Farewell and Thank You

Thank you for joining me on this exploration of MS-DOS. I hope this book has empowered you to not only master the operating system but also to appreciate its historical significance and lasting impact. Farewell, and may your future endeavors in the realm of technology be filled with curiosity, discovery, and a thirst for knowledge.

Addendum

Memory Management Notes

Memory Managers

the memory manager holds a crucial responsibility – overseeing the allocation and utilization of system memory. It acts as a central authority, ensuring each program receives the memory it needs to run effectively while preventing conflicts and maximizing efficiency. The memory manager fulfills two central functions:

When a program launches, it requires dedicated space in memory to store its instructions and data. The memory manager maintains a detailed record of all memory locations in a data structure called a "memory map." This map acts as an inventory, indicating which areas are currently occupied and by which programs. If free memory exists, the manager allocates a suitable block to the requesting program and updates the memory map accordingly.
The memory manager meticulously tracks which programs occupy specific memory locations. This information is essential for preventing conflicts and ensuring smooth operation. It constantly monitors memory usage and maintains a record of which programs are utilizing specific areas.

Preventing Memory Conflicts:

Memory conflicts can occur when two programs attempt to access the same location simultaneously. This can lead to data corruption or program crashes. The memory manager plays a vital role in preventing such situations. By leveraging its tracking data, it can identify potential clashes. When a conflict is detected, the manager can take steps to prevent it, such as temporarily blocking one program's access until the other finishes using the shared memory location. This ensures orderly access and safeguards data integrity.

Optimizing Memory Usage for Performance:

Beyond allocation and conflict resolution, memory managers strive for optimal memory utilization. One technique employed is memory compaction. This process involves rearranging programs within memory to consolidate free memory blocks into contiguous chunks. Fragmentation occurs when free memory becomes scattered throughout the address space in small, unusable pockets. Compaction helps to alleviate this issue, improving overall system performance by reducing the time it takes programs to access the data they need.

MS-DOS memory management witnessed the rise of various memory managers, each addressing specific needs and offering unique advantages. Here's an exploration of some prominent contenders:

- **QEMM (Quarterdeck Expanded Memory Manager):** A pioneer in the memory management arena, QEMM carved a niche by introducing features absent from the base MS-DOS. Notably, it unlocked access to extended memory, a vast reservoir beyond the conventional memory limitations. Additionally, QEMM empowered users with the ability to create Upper Memory Blocks (UMBs). These special regions within the first megabyte of memory allowed for the storage of device drivers and memory-resident programs, freeing up precious conventional memory for applications. QEMM's innovative features and user-friendliness propelled it to become a widely adopted solution.

- **EMM386 (Expanded Memory Manager 386):** EMM386 emerged as another popular contender, boasting a feature set comparable to QEMM. However, it distinguished itself by exhibiting superior compatibility with newer MS-DOS iterations. Furthermore, EMM386 demonstrated greater efficiency in memory management, making it a compelling choice for systems with limited memory resources. This combination of compatibility and efficiency solidified EMM386's position as a trusted memory management solution.

- **386MAX:** Designed to surpass the capabilities of QEMM and EMM386, 386MAX offered a more robust and versatile feature set. It catered to users seeking a wider range of functionalities, including the ability to emulate expanded memory for programs lacking native support. Additionally, 386MAX boasted improved efficiency compared to its predecessors. However, this enhanced power came at the cost of increased complexity in configuration. Users willing to invest time in configuration could unlock significant memory management benefits with 386MAX.

- **DOS/4GW:** This memory manager aimed to bridge the gap between MS-DOS and Windows 3.1 by offering compatibility with both operating systems. While sharing a similar feature set with QEMM and EMM386, DOS/4GW excelled in compatibility with newer versions of MS-DOS and Windows. This compatibility made it an ideal choice for users who frequently switched between these environments.

- **UMBPCI (Upper Memory Block for PCI):** UMBPCI addressed a specific niche in memory management. It focused on utilizing unused memory blocks originally reserved for PCI expansion cards. By leveraging this untapped resource, UMBPCI could create Upper Memory Blocks. This approach proved beneficial for freeing up conventional memory for DOS applications, potentially leading to performance improvements. UMBPCI catered particularly to users with older computers struggling with limited memory resources.

Expanded Memory Vs. Extended Memory

What is Expanded Memory In MS DOS?

in the era of MS DOS conventional memory was limited to 640 kilobytes which posed a significant constraint for running increasingly sophisticated applications expanded memory emerged as a clever solution to circumvent this limitation allowing DOS programs to access additional memory beyond the conventional 640 kilobyte boundary expanded memory is a memory management technique called Bank switching that allows DOS programs to access more memory than the 640k limit it works by dividing the Upper Memory Area into Pages. Pages of expanded memory can then be swapped in and out of the page frame as needed. This page swapping mechanism enables DOS programs to access more memory enhancing their overall performance
Expanded memory was developed in the late 1980s as a way to allow DOS programs to take advantage of the increasing amount of memory that was becoming available in personal computers. It was widely used by many popular DOS programs including games databases and spreadsheets.

Advantages of Expanded Memory

Expanded memory offered several advantages for dos users it allowed dos programs to handle larger data sets complex operations and more advanced Graphics effectively expanding the capabilities of Dos software multitasking was also improved by providing more memory for multiple applications allowing users to run several dos programs simultaneously without significant performance degradation

Use Expanded Memory When :

You would use expanded memory on MS DOS when you need to run a DOS program that requires more memory than the 640 kilobyte limit. Expanded memory is also useful for running multiple DOS programs at the same time because it allows each program to have its own dedicated memory space. Expanded memory was also compatible with a wide range of popular dos programs making it a practical solution for many users without requiring significant changes to their existing software. Here are some specific examples of when you would use expanded memory. Running a spreadsheet program with a large data set like Lotus 123 or Microsoft Excel, running a database program with a large number of Records like dBase 4 or Paradox, running a word processing program with a large document like WordPerfect or Microsoft Word, running games like Wing Commander Doom or Wolfenstein 3D or running multiple dos programs at the same time expanded memory played a crucial role in overcoming the memory limitations of MS DOS providing a practical solution for users seeking to run more demanding applications and enhance their overall Computing experience while expanded memory was eventually superseded by extended memory it remains a significant milestone in the evolution of DOS memory management

What Is Extended Memory in MS-DOS?

extended memory in MS DOS refers to memory that resides above the first megabyte of address space, a realm previously inaccessible to Conventional DOS programs. Extended memory can be accessed by DOS programs running and protect protected mode a more advanced operating mode that enabled direct access to memory beyond the conventional boundary this allowed for significantly larger memory allocations enabling dos programs to handle more complex tasks and utilize Advanced features

Use Extended Memory When:

You would use extended memory on MS-DOS when you need to run a DOS program that requires access to more than 1 Megabyte of memory. Extended memory is also useful for for running dos programs that need to use high performance devices such as network adapters and CD-ROM drives. Extended memory is used by DOS programs in a variety of ways including to store data and code to create buffers for data that is being transferred between devices or to load drivers that are too large to fit into conventional memory. This allows DOS programs to use devices such as network adapters and CD-ROM drives here are some specific examples when you would use extended memory running a game with high quality graphics and sound effects, running a DOSprogram that uses a high performance device such as a network adapter or CD- ROM drive, or running a DOS program that is too large to fit in conventional memory

What is The Difference Between Expanded Memory and Extended Memory in MS DOS?

The main difference between expanded and extended memory in MS-DOS is that expanded memory is emulated within the first 1 Megabyte of address space while extended memory is physically above the 1 Megabyte address boundary. Expanded memory can be used by DOS programs running in real mode and is accessed through a special page frame which can slow down performance. Extended memory can only be used by DOS programs running in protected mode. It is typically much faster than expanded memory because it is accessed directly by the processor. It can get confusing when talking about expanded memory and extended memory because the words are very similar. Actually only two letters are different thankfully the abbreviations are a little easier to tell apart expanded memory is abbreviated as EMS extended memory is abbreviated as XMS

How to Enable EMS

To enable EMS we need to load a memory manager. The most common memory manager you'll find is the one included in MS DOS called EMM386. `EMM386.EXE` can be loaded from the `CONFIG.SYS` file with the argument `RAM` which specifies a range of segment addresses to be used for upper memory blocks and enables EMS support. If you do not specify a range EMM386 uses all available adapter space to create upper memory blocks and a page frame for EMS.

How to Enable XMS

To enable XMS use the `NOEMS` argument for `EMM386.EXE` which provides access to the upper memory area but prevents access to expanded memory. Using the `NOEMS` argument is a generally good configuration unless you plan on using very old MS-DOS software in which case you may want to set up a boot men u to easily switch between configurations or use a boot disk specifically designed for the software you want to use

`CONFIG.SYS` and `AUTOEXEC.BAT` Considerations

During my exploration of classic games for this book, I encountered a few peculiar crashes that stemmed from overly ambitious memory management settings. Initially, I opted for a more aggressive approach, aiming to maximize available conventional memory through adjustments to parameters like `FILES`, `STACKS`, and `FCBS`. These settings dictate factors like the number of open files, program stacks, and file control blocks – all critical for system operation, but also memory consumers.

However, while this approach liberated more memory on paper, it came at the cost of unforeseen stability issues in some games. Random crashes became a recurring nuisance, hindering my ability to thoroughly test and enjoy these titles. This experience highlighted the importance of striking a balance between maximizing memory utilization and ensuring system stability.

The solution arrived in the form of a more conservative set of memory management parameters. As detailed below, I now utilize:

`FILES=40` : This allows for a reasonable number of simultaneously open files, catering to most applications without being excessive.

`BUFFERS=10,0` : This configuration optimizes disk caching for my specific setup.

`FCBS=1` : This maintains a single file control block, which is generally sufficient for most DOS operations.

`STACKS=9,128` : This allocates nine program stacks, each with a size of 128 KB. This provides adequate stack space for most applications while not claiming an exorbitant amount of memory.

While this revised approach consumes a few additional kilobytes of conventional memory compared to the initial aggressive settings, the trade-off is undeniably worthwhile. The newfound stability ensures smoother gameplay and a more reliable testing environment for the games featured in this book.

Furthermore, the implementation of boot menus, as described later, allows for multiple memory configurations. This empowers me to temporarily adjust settings for particularly memory-intensive games, essentially having the best of both worlds: a stable system for everyday use and the ability to liberate additional memory when absolutely necessary.

Optimizing Performance with Advanced Driver Configuration (Technical Note)

While the default configuration of MSCDEX and SmartDrive provides adequate functionality, for power users seeking to squeeze out the most performance and memory efficiency, advanced configuration options exist. Here's a breakdown of the parameters mentioned:

```
LOADHIGH C:\DOS\MSCDEX.EXE /D:MSCD001 /L:F /E
/M:30
LOADHIGH C:\DOS\SMARTDRV.EXE 4096 4096 /B:65536
/E:8192 /U
```

MSCDEX.EXE
/e : This parameter instructs MSCDEX to utilize expanded memory (provided by a memory manager like EMM386.EXE) for caching data. This offloads data storage from precious conventional memory, potentially improving overall system performance.
/m:30 : This parameter specifies the number of buffers MSCDEX will utilize for caching data. A higher value, like 30 in this case, translates to a larger cache but also consumes more expanded memory. This can significantly reduce the number of direct CD-ROM reads required, leading to faster access times.
Important Note: Utilizing the /e parameter requires a functional EMM386.EXE memory manager. Without it, the /e parameter will be ignored. Additionally, using /m:30 without EMM386 will significantly increase conventional memory usage. In such scenarios, it's recommended to lower the cache size by adjusting /m to a value like 5 or 10 to minimize conventional memory footprint.
SmartDrive.EXE:
4096 4096 : These parameters define the initial and maximum cache sizes for SmartDrive, measured in bytes. Adjusting these values can influence performance and memory usage. A larger cache can improve performance but consumes more conventional memory. Experimentation might be necessary to find the optimal balance for your specific needs.
/b:65536 : This parameter sets the buffer size for SmartDrive, also measured in bytes. A larger buffer size can potentially improve efficiency, but again, it consumes more conventional memory.

/e:8192 : This parameter instructs SmartDrive to utilize expanded memory (similar to /e with MSCDEX) for caching data, reducing the impact on conventional memory. However, it requires a functional EMM386.EXE memory manager.

/u: This parameter enables write-behind caching, a technique where data modifications are not immediately written back to the disk but stored in the cache for later flushing. While this can improve performance, it introduces a slight risk of data loss in case of a system crash before the data is written back.

Simplifying Configuration with Boot Menus in MS-DOS

MS-DOS 6.0 marked a pivotal moment in user experience with the introduction of boot menus. This groundbreaking feature revolutionized how users managed system configurations, particularly for those juggling multiple settings tailored for various purposes.

Prior to this innovation, modifying system behavior relied heavily on editing arcane configuration files like CONFIG.SYS and AUTOEXEC.BAT. This process could be tedious and error-prone, especially for users who frequently switched between settings depending on their needs. Tasks like optimizing memory allocation for different applications or loading specific drivers for games often necessitated manual configuration file edits.

Boot menus elegantly addressed this challenge by introducing a user-friendly interface. During system startup, a menu displaying pre-configured options would appear. Users could simply select the desired configuration, eliminating the need for direct manipulation of cryptic text files.

Imagine a scenario: You have a computer loaded with a diverse library of games, each requiring specific memory allocation or peripheral drivers to run smoothly. Traditionally, you might have resorted to creating individual boot disks for each game, each containing the customized configuration files. This approach was not only cumbersome but also prone to physical disk wear and potential mismanagement. Boot menus offered a far more elegant solution.

By creating separate boot menu entries, each meticulously tailored to a specific game's requirements, users could effortlessly switch between configurations at boot time. This eliminated the need for a plethora of boot disks or the constant tinkering with configuration files.

Furthermore, manually editing configuration files carried an inherent risk of introducing errors. A misplaced semicolon or a typographical mistake could render your system unstable, leading to frustrating troubleshooting sessions. Boot menus provided a safer and more intuitive approach. By selecting pre-defined settings from a user-friendly interface, the risk of errors associated with direct file manipulation was significantly reduced.

While not essential for every user, boot menus offered a significant convenience factor for those managing diverse system configurations. Let's look at the basics of building a boot menu

1. Edit your CONFIG.SYS file.
2. Add a new section named "[menu]" at the beginning of your CONFIG.SYS file. This tells the system you're using a boot menu.

106

3. Within the "[menu]" section, use the following commands:

    1. **Menucolor:** (Optional) This sets the text and background colors for the menu screen. You can choose from various color codes (refer to the book for details).

    2. **Menudefault:** (Optional) This specifies the default configuration to load if no selection is made within a certain time (also set here) during startup.

    3. **Menuitem:** This defines an item on the boot menu. Use this command for each configuration you want to include. It takes two parts:

        1. **blockname:** The exact name of the corresponding configuration section within your CONFIG.SYS file.

        2. **menu_text:** (Optional) The text displayed on the menu for this configuration. If not provided, the blockname will be used.

Example:

```
[MENU]   ; Start of menu section
MENUCOLOR=15,1   ; Bright white text on blue
background
MENUDEFAULT=Games,10   ; Load "Games" config by
default after 10 seconds
MENUITEM=Games,Games with Soundcard   ; Menu text
for "Games" config
MENUITEM=Work   ; Menu text for "Work" config
(block name used)
```

Save your modified CONFIG.SYS file and restart your computer. You should now see a boot menu with the options you defined. Simply choose the desired configuration and your system will load it automatically.

The previous section provided a basic framework for creating a boot menu in MS-DOS. While that approach offers a significant improvement in managing configurations, some users might crave even finer control over their system's behavior. This section delves into a more intricate example (for illustrative purposes only) showcasing how boot menus can be leveraged to tailor settings for specific games.

Note: This example is quite complex and likely exceeds the needs of most users. Consider it a reference point for understanding the extensive customization possibilities offered by boot menus in MS-DOS

Optimizing for Every Game:

The provided configuration files demonstrate a setup geared towards achieving the most optimal settings for a wide variety of games. While the "default" configuration might suffice for most titles, individual entries are created for many games, allowing for meticulous fine-tuning.

Is it Necessary?: It's crucial to understand that this level of customization is not essential for everyone. Many users can enjoy a great gaming experience with a well-defined "default" configuration. However, for those seeking to squeeze every ounce of performance out of their system for specific titles, boot menus offer a powerful tool to achieve this goal.

Learning from the Example: While directly implementing this complex example might not be necessary, it serves as a valuable illustration. By studying the structure of the configuration files and the specific commands used for each game, you can gain valuable insights into how to optimize your own system for the games you play most. Remember, the core concepts remain the same – defining configurations, building the boot menu, and leveraging menu options. This example simply pushes those concepts to their limits, demonstrating the remarkable level of control achievable through boot menus in MS-DOS.

Overly Complicated `CONFIG.SYS` file:

```
REM Configure boot menu
[MENU]
MENUITEM=default,Load standard MS-DOS 6.22 working
environment
SUBMENU=games1,Load gaming-optimized environment
MENUDEFAULT=default,5
REM prompt for game-focused options
[GAMES1]
SUBMENU=GAMES2,Basic optimizations - Disable EMS,
disable CD-ROM
MENUITEM=-EMS+CD,Wing Commander III/IV, Crusader,
SkyNET - Disable EMS, enable CD-ROM
MENUITEM=-EMS+CD_MAX,Privateer 2 - Disable EMS,
enable CD-ROM, extreme optimization
MENUITEM=+EMS_MAX,Wing Commander I/II - Enable
EMS, perform extreme optimizations
MENUITEM=+EMS+CD-M-SD,Tomb Raider - Enable EMS and
CD-ROM, Disable Mouse and SmartDrive
```

```
REM prompt for additional game options
[GAMES2]
MENUITEM=basic,All other games - Basic
optimizations only
MENUITEM=-EMS-SD,Dark Forces - Disable SmartDrive
MENUITEM=-EMS_MAX,Privateer 1 - Perform extreme
optimizations
REM common boot/memory settings - always enable
XMS
[COMMON]
SWITCHES=/F
DEVICE=C:\DOS\HIMEM.SYS /TESTMEM:OFF
REM Enable EMS for default environment or games
that require it
[DEFAULT]
DEVICE=C:\DOS\EMM386.EXE RAM 24576 HIGHSCAN NOTR
I=B000-B7FF
DOS=HIGH,UMB
DEVICEHIGH=C:\DOS\POWER.EXE ADV:MIN
INSTALLHIGH=C:\APPS\ANSIPLUS\ANSIPLUS.EXE /E
DEVICEHIGH=C:\DOS\CDROMDRV.SYS /D:MSCD001
SHELL=C:\APPS\4DOS\4DOS.COM C:\APPS\4DOS /P
[+EMS_MAX]
DEVICE=C:\DOS\EMM386.EXE RAM 24576 HIGHSCAN NOTR
I=B000-B7FF
DOS=HIGH,UMB
SHELL=C:\DOS\COMMAND.COM C:\DOS /P
[+EMS+CD-M-SD]
DEVICE=C:\DOS\EMM386.EXE RAM 24576 HIGHSCAN NOTR
I=B000-B7FF
DOS=HIGH,UMB
DEVICE=C:\DOS\CDROMDRV.SYS /D:MSCD001
DEVICEHIGH=C:\DOS\ANSI.SYS
SHELL=C:\APPS\4DOS\4DOS.COM C:\APPS\4DOS /P
REM Disable EMS for all other games
[BASIC]
DOS=HIGH
DEVICE=C:\DOS\ANSI.SYS
```

```
SHELL=C:\APPS\4DOS\4DOS.COM C:\APPS\4DOS /P
[-EMS+CD]
DOS=HIGH
DEVICE=C:\DOS\ANSI.SYS
DEVICE=C:\DOS\CDROMDRV.SYS /D:MSCD001
SHELL=C:\APPS\4DOS\4DOS.COM C:\APPS\4DOS /P
[-EMS+CD_MAX]
DOS=HIGH
DEVICE=C:\DOS\CDROMDRV.SYS /D:MSCD001
SHELL=C:\DOS\COMMAND.COM C:\DOS /P
[-EMS-SD]
DOS=HIGH
DEVICE=C:\DOS\ANSI.SYS
SHELL=C:\APPS\4DOS\4DOS.COM C:\APPS\4DOS /P
[-EMS_MAX]
DOS=HIGH
SHELL=C:\DOS\COMMAND.COM C:\DOS /P
REM Configure remaining drivers and default
environmental settings
[COMMON]
DEVICE=C:\APPS\CTCM\CTCM.EXE
FILES=40
BUFFERS=10,0
FCBS=1
STACKS=9,128
LASTDRIVE=H
BREAK=ON
```

C orresponding AUTOEXEC.BAT file:

```
@ECHO OFF
:: Configure environment based on config.sys menu
selection
GOTO %CONFIG%
:: For default working environment, load all
conveniences
:DEFAULT
```

110

```
C:\APPS\ANSIPLUS\SETAPLUS.EXE MODE 03H HEIGHT 8
RATE 30 DELAY 1
LOADHIGH C:\DOS\MSCDEX.EXE /D:MSCD001 /L:F /E
/M:30
LOADHIGH C:\DOS\SMARTDRV.EXE 4096 4096 /B:65536
/E:8192 /U
C:\DOS\CTMOUSE.EXE /3 /O
PROMPT $E[1;34M$P$G $E[0;47;0M
ALIAS /R D:\ETC\ALIASES.CFG
GOTO NETWORK
:: For gaming environment, load memory-optimized
configuration
:BASIC
C:\DOS\MODE.COM CON: COLS=80 LINES=50 RATE=32
DELAY=1
C:\DOS\SMARTDRV.EXE 2048 2048 /B:32768 /E:8192 /U
C:\DOS\CTMOUSE.EXE /3 /O
PROMPT $E[1;34M$P$G $E[0;47;0M
ALIAS /R D:\ETC\ALIASES.CFG
GOTO FINISH
:: Otherwise, apply more specialized settings
:-EMS+CD
C:\DOS\MSCDEX.EXE /D:MSCD001 /L:F /M:20
C:\DOS\SMARTDRV.EXE 4096 4096 /B:32768 /E:8192 /U
C:\DOS\CTMOUSE.EXE /3 /O
PROMPT $E[1;34M$P$G $E[0;47;0M
ALIAS /R D:\ETC\ALIASES.CFG
GOTO FINISH
:-EMS+CD_MAX
C:\DOS\MSCDEX.EXE /D:MSCD001 /L:F /M:5
C:\DOS\SMARTDRV.EXE 2048 2048 /B:2048 /E:1024 /U
C:\DOS\CTMOUSE.EXE /3 /O
PROMPT $P$G
GOTO FINISH
:+EMS_MAX
LOADHIGH C:\DOS\SMARTDRV.EXE 4096 4096 /B:32768
/E:8192 /U
```

```
C:\DOS\CTMOUSE.EXE /3 /O
PROMPT $P$G
GOTO FINISH
:+EMS+CD-M-SD
C:\DOS\MSCDEX.EXE /D:MSCD001 /L:F /M:20
PROMPT $E[1;34M$P$G $E[0;47;0M
ALIAS /R D:\ETC\ALIASES.CFG
GOTO FINISH
:-EMS-SD
C:\DOS\CTMOUSE.EXE /3 /O
PROMPT $E[1;34M$P$G $E[0;47;0M
ALIAS /R D:\ETC\ALIASES.CFG
GOTO FINISH
:-EMS_MAX
C:\DOS\SMARTDRV.EXE 2048 2048 /B:4096 /E:2048 /U
C:\DOS\CTMOUSE.EXE /3 /O
PROMPT $P$G
GOTO FINISH

:: Load Network Drivers And Configure Protocol
Stacks
:NETWORK
ECHO.
ECHO INITIALIZING 3COM 3C509B-TPO...
LOADHIGH C:\DOS\3C509.COM -P 0X60 >NUL
ECHO.
ECHO SETTING MTCP IP ADDRESS VIA DHCP...
SET MTCPCFG=D:\ETC\MTCP.CFG
SET TZ=CST6CDT
C:\APPS\DHCP.EXE >NUL
ECHO SETTING SYSTEM TIME VIA NTP...
C:\APPS\SNTP.EXE -SET BOXDOG.LEGROOM.NET >NUL
SET WATTCP.CFG=D:\ETC
GOTO FINISH
:: Configure remaining common drivers and
environmental variables
:FINISH
ECHO.
```

```
ECHO INITIALIZING CREATIVE LABS SOUND BLASTER
AWE64...
SET SOUND=C:\APPS\AWE64
SET BLASTER=A220 I5 D1 H5 P330 E620 T6
SET MIDI=SYNTH:1 MAP:E MODE:0
SET CTCM=C:\APPS\CTCM
C:\APPS\AWE64\DIAGNOSE.EXE /S >NUL
C:\APPS\AWE64\AWEUTIL.COM /S >NUL
C:\APPS\AWE64\MIXERSET.EXE /P /Q
C:\APPS\CTCM\CTCM.EXE /S >NUL
UNSET CTCM
PATH C:\APPS;C:\DOS
SET DIRCMD=/A/O:GNE
SET TEMP=C:\TEMP
ECHO.
```

AUTOEXEC.BAT File Deep Dive:

The unassuming AUTOEXEC.BAT file is a cornerstone of MS-DOS. It's your personal launchpad, acting behind the scenes every time you boot your system. This file holds immense power, allowing you to automate a myriad of tasks and configure your MS-DOS environment to your exact preferences.

Whether you're a seasoned MS-DOS user or just starting your journey, this section delves into the intricate workings of AUTOEXEC.BAT. We'll explore a comprehensive range of commands you can leverage to customize your boot process, optimize performance, and tailor your MS-DOS experience to your specific needs.

So, grab your favorite text editor and prepare to embark on a deep dive into the fascinating world of AUTOEXEC.BAT! We'll dissect various commands, explore their functionalities, and provide practical examples to illuminate their usage. By the end of this chapter, you'll be a master of crafting a powerful and personalized AUTOEXEC.BAT file, transforming your MS-DOS environment into a well-oiled and efficient machine.

One of the most common lines you'll encounter at the beginning of this file is `@ECHO OFF`.

```
@ECHO OFF
```

The `ECHO` command in MS-DOS serves a simple yet significant function: controlling the display of information on the screen. It possesses three primary parameters:

On: When used as `ECHO ON`, it instructs the operating system to display all subsequent commands entered on the command line, including those within batch files like

`AUTOEXEC.BAT` . This can be helpful for debugging purposes, as it allows you to visualize the execution flow.

Off: Conversely, `ECHO OFF` silences the output. Commands within the batch file, such as loading device drivers or setting environment variables, are executed silently without cluttering the screen with unnecessary text.

Message: The `ECHO` command can also be used to display custom messages on the screen. For instance, `ECHO Welcome to your MS-DOS System!` would print that specific message during execution.

By placing `@ECHO OFF` at the beginning of your `AUTOEXEC.BAT` file, you achieve two key benefits:

Enhanced Boot Screen Aesthetics: During system startup, various commands from `AUTOEXEC.BAT` are executed in sequence. Without `@ECHO OFF` , each command would be displayed on the screen, creating a cluttered and potentially confusing display for the user. `@ECHO OFF` ensures a clean boot screen, showing only essential system messages, such as those related to hardware detection or memory management.

Improved Performance (Minimal): While the performance gain is relatively small, suppressing the output of commands can lead to a slightly faster boot process. This is because the system doesn't need to spend time displaying each command on the screen before executing the next one.

In essence, `@ECHO OFF` contributes to a more user-friendly and efficient boot experience in MS-DOS by ensuring a clean boot screen and potentially offering a minor performance boost.

Understanding Environment Variable

In MS-DOS, the SET command within your AUTOEXEC.BAT file plays a crucial role in defining and managing environment variables. These variables act like named shortcuts that point to specific locations or settings on your system. They offer a convenient way for programs and the MS-DOS shell itself to access frequently used data without requiring you to specify the entire path or value every single time.

The basic syntax for the SET command is: SET <variable_name>=<value>

```
SET TEMP=C:\TEMP
```

Explanation:
<variable_name>: This is the name you assign to the environment variable. It should be a descriptive and unique name e.g. TEMP.
<value>: This is the data you associate with the variable. It can be a path to a directory, a filename, a numerical value, or even a string of text.

T he `PATH` environment variable plays a pivotal role in locating and executing programs from the command prompt. It functions like a roadmap, guiding the operating system to the specific directories where executable files (often with the `.COM` or `.EXE` extensions) reside.

Imagine typing `EDIT` at the command prompt. Without a defined PATH, MS-DOS searches only the current directory for the edit program. If edit resides in a different directory, like `C:\DOS\`, you'll encounter the error message "Bad command or file name." This is because the current directory might be the root of your C drive (e.g., `C:\`), and searching only there yields no results.

To ensure seamless program execution, it's essential to define the `PATH` in your `AUTOEXEC.BAT` file. This file automatically executes commands each time you start the PC, and setting the `PATH` here establishes the search locations for executable files from the outset.

Common Locations for Program Directories: Here are some common directories you might include in your `PATH`:

`C:\` : The root directory of your C drive.

`C:\DOS` : The directory containing core MS-DOS system files, often including utilities like `EDIT`.

`C:\WINDOWS` : If you have Windows installed on your system, the Windows directory might house various executable programs.

Adding Multiple Paths and Character Limitations: You can include multiple directories in your `PATH` statement, separated by semicolons (;). However, there's a crucial limitation – the total PATH length cannot exceed 122 characters. This might pose a challenge if you have a large number of program directories scattered across your system.

Next Let's delve into two noteworthy environment variables and how they enhance your MS-DOS experience:

COMSPEC: This crucial variable dictates the location of the `COMMAND.COM` file, the core interpreter responsible for processing your commands in MS-DOS. By specifying the path to `COMMAND.COM` within the `COMSPEC` variable, the system knows precisely where to locate this essential program for command execution.

TEMP: The `TEMP` variable designates a dedicated directory for storing temporary files created by MS-DOS and other programs. These temporary files often hold transient data used during program execution and are typically discarded upon program termination. Specifying a `TEMP` directory ensures these temporary files are stored in a designated location, promoting a more organized system.

Example: Setting the TEMP Variable

The provided line in your `AUTOEXEC.BAT` file, `SET TEMP=C:\TEMP`, exemplifies setting the `TEMP` environment variable. Here's a breakdown of what this line accomplishes:

`SET` : This keyword initiates the process of setting an environment variable.

`TEMP` : This specifies the name of the environment variable being modified, which in this case is `TEMP`.

`C:\TEMP` : This defines the value assigned to the TEMP variable. It indicates that the `C:\TEMP` directory will be used to store temporary files.

Imagine having a customizable banner that displays helpful information right at your fingertips. That's precisely what the `PROMPT` command allows you to achieve. By entering specific codes within the `SET PROMPT` command in your `AUTOEXEC.BAT` file, you can modify the information displayed at the prompt.
Here's a breakdown of some commonly used codes:

`$P` : This code displays the current drive letter and directory path. For instance, if you're in the `C:\USERS\USERNAME\DOCUMENTS` directory, the prompt will show `C:\USERS\USERNAME\DOCUMENTS`
`$G` : This ubiquitous greater than sign (>) serves as the standard prompt ending, indicating you're ready to enter a command.

example:
By entering `SET PROMPT=$P$G` in your `AUTOEXEC.BAT` file, you achieve the default prompt behavior, displaying the current drive and directory followed by the greater than sign.
However, the power of `PROMPT` lies in its versatility. Suppose you'd like to see the current date and time alongside your directory path. You can achieve this by incorporating the `$D` (date) and `$T` (time) codes:

```
SET PROMPT=$P $D $T $G
```

This modified prompt would display something like `C:\APPS 03-15-2024 20:40:00 >` (assuming the current date and time are March 15, 2024, and 8:40 PM).

Terminate-and-Stay-Resident (TSR) Programs

Now let's delve into the world of TSRs (Terminate-and-Stay-Resident) programs and how to optimize their loading using your `AUTOEXEC.BAT` file. TSRs are a unique type of program that remain resident in memory even after they've finished their initial task. Common examples include MSCDEX for CD-ROM access and mouse drivers.

Benefits of Loading TSRs High: By default, DOS loads programs into conventional memory, a limited space crucial for running applications. However, we can leverage a technique called loading high to place TSRs in a special area called Upper Memory Blocks (UMBs). This offers significant advantages:

Frees Up Conventional Memory: By placing TSRs in UMBs, we reclaim valuable conventional memory for applications that require it directly. This can improve overall system performance and stability.

Improves Memory Management: With fewer programs occupying conventional memory, managing memory becomes easier. This can minimize conflicts and ensure smoother operation.

Example:

Here's how to load common TSRs like MSCDEX and mouse drivers high using your `AUTOEXEC.BAT` file. The key to loading high lies in the `LH` command. Include this line in your `AUTOEXEC.BAT` file, followed by the path to the TSR's executable file.

For MSCDEX, you'll also need to define the target drive using the `/d:` switch followed by the drive letter assigned to your CD-ROM drive (ensure it matches the configuration in `CONFIG.SYS`). Similar to MSCDEX, use the `LH` command followed by the path to your mouse driver's executable file.

```
LH C:\DOS\MSCDEX.EXE /D:MSCD001
LH C:\DOS\MOUSE.COM
```

The Power of DOSKEY:

While MS-DOS boasts a robust command line interface, it can sometimes feel rigid compared to modern operating systems. Fear not! Utilities like DOSKEY can breathe new life into your MS-DOS experience, transforming it into a more user-friendly and efficient environment.
DOSKEY is a TSR (Terminate and Stay Resident) program, meaning it loads into memory and remains active in the background. This allows it to offer a variety of features that significantly enhance your command line interactions:

DOSKEY keeps a running log of your previously entered commands. No more frantically trying to remember that complex command you used earlier! Simply use the up and down arrow keys to navigate through your command history, select the desired entry, and press Enter to execute it again. This saves you time and eliminates the frustration of retyping long commands.
Made a typo in a command? No sweat! DOSKEY allows you to edit previously entered commands using the familiar left and right arrow keys. Once you've positioned the cursor at the error, use the Backspace or Delete key to fix your mistake. This eliminates the need to start from scratch, streamlining your workflow.
Imagine effortlessly launching your favorite programs or frequently used commands with a single, short alias. DOSKEY lets you define aliases, acting like nicknames for longer commands. For instance, you could create an alias named "DIRLONG" that executes the command "DIR /W /P", displaying a directory listing with wide file names and pausing at the end of each screen. This saves you time and keeps your most used commands readily accessible.

These are just a few of the ways DOSKEY empowers you to work with the MS-DOS command line more effectively. Let's look at a practical example:
Suppose you're working on a project that involves frequent directory changes and file listing. You can create a DOSKEY macro to automate this process. A macro is a series of commands grouped under a single name. Here's an example macro named "DIRLONG" that combines directory change and a detailed listing:

```
DOSKEY DIRLONG=CD C:\PROJECTS\MYPROJECT & DIR
/W /P
```

explanation:
Now, whenever you type "DIRLONG" and press Enter, DOSKEY will first change the directory to "C:\PROJECTS\MYPROJECT" and then execute the "DIR /W /P" command, providing you with a wide listing of the files within that directory.

Fine-Tuning Keyboard Response with MODE

The MODE command offers a surprising degree of control over your keyboard behavior. Beyond basic configuration of communication ports and the display, it allows you to modify the keyboard's typematic rate – how quickly characters repeat when a key is held down.
This can be particularly beneficial for users who find the default repeat rate too slow or too fast. The MODE command accepts two values for typematic rate adjustment:

Repetition Speed. The first value you set determines how quickly characters repeat. Lower numbers make them repeat faster, while higher numbers slow it down.
Initial Delay. The second value controls the delay before a key starts repeating. A higher value here introduces a short pause before the characters fire off in rapid succession.

Example: To configure a faster typematic rate with a minimal delay, you could use the following command in your AUTOEXEC.BAT file:

```
MODE CON LINES=1 COLUMNS=80 RATE=300 DELAY=1
```

This adjusts the console window to 80 columns for improved readability (standard is 40) and sets the typematic rate to 300 characters per second with a 1-millisecond delay.

Expanding File Accessibility with APPEND

Similar to the PATH environment variable, which tells MS-DOS where to locate executable programs, the APPEND command serves a complementary purpose for text files. It allows you to define additional directories where the operating system will search for text files when using commands like TYPE .

Example: Imagine you have a dedicated data directory named `C:\MYDATA` where you store various text files. By adding the following line to your `AUTOEXEC.BAT` file:

```
APPEND C:\MYDATA
```

Now, you can simply use `TYPE` followed by the filename (e.g., `TYPE MYREPORT.TXT`) to view the contents of `MYREPORT.TXT` residing in `C:\MYDATA` without needing to specify the full path. This simplifies file access and streamlines your workflow.

Modular Network Configuration with Batch File Calls

The beauty of `AUTOEXEC.BAT` lies in its ability to execute other batch files. This proves particularly useful when setting up network configurations in MS-DOS. Instead of cluttering your `AUTOEXEC.BAT` file with a lengthy sequence of network-related commands, you can leverage batch file calls.

Example: Create a separate batch file named `NETSETUP.BAT` containing all the commands necessary for loading network drivers and establishing network connectivity. Then, within your `AUTOEXEC.BAT` file, simply include a line like:

```
CALL NETSETUP.BAT
```

This approach promotes modularity and organization. Your `AUTOEXEC.BAT` file remains clean and focused on core system settings, while the network configuration specifics reside in a dedicated and easily maintainable batch file (`NETSETUP.BAT`).

www.ingramcontent.com/pod-product-compliance
Lightning Source LLC
Chambersburg PA
CBHW080538060326
40690CB00022B/5171